THE FIRST FIFTY YEARS

CARL WITTKE

THE FIRST FIFTY YEARS

The Cleveland Museum of Art

1916–1966

A JOINT PUBLICATION

The John Huntington Art and Polytechnic Trust

The Cleveland Museum of Art

Trustees

Foreword

THE HISTORY AND organization of art museums, here and abroad, is a mystery to many, and but moderately well known to a few. Publicly-owned, that is state, museums are taken for granted abroad and also include many of the most famous museums of America—the National Gallery in Washington, the Detroit Institute of Arts, the City Art Museum of St. Louis, to name only a few. But even these have private support to greater or lesser degree. What is less understood is that some of the major art museums of America are completely privately-owned, non-profit corporations or institutions for the public good; one thinks of the Museum of Fine Arts, Boston, the Toledo Art Museum, the William Rockhill Nelson Gallery of Art in Kansas City, and of our own museum, The Cleveland Museum of Art. The history of these latter institutions is known to their trustees, members and close friends; but it is not at all familiar to others, and much confusion and misunderstanding results from lack of information. *The First Fifty Years* is one concrete effort to clarify and add to the record, on this, our fiftieth anniversary.

The private and independent institution for the pursuit of excellence and *pro bono publico* is well known through many American schools, colleges, universities, and libraries. Such names as Harvard, Yale, Vassar, Smith, Stanford, Carnegie,

v

Loeb, and others are as familiar, or more so, as institutions as they are as names of the individuals associated with them. These institutions have justly achieved their fame by proving that the public good is usually best served by excellence rather than expediency, by action following reflection rather than pressure, and by a knowing variety of tradition rather than a blind conformity to the unity of fashion. Many of these institutions have well-published histories revealing their varied fortunes and the ways by which they developed their present form. Such histories are a part of the social history of our country, and are little known or understood.

In adding a history of The Cleveland Museum of Art to others we have been fortunate to have as our historian Dr. Carl Wittke, formerly Dean of the Graduate School of Western Reserve University, and an eminent scholar of social history. Dean Wittke has written the story of the Museum from a regional as well as from a national and international viewpoint. He has purposely emphasized those historical, social, legal, economic, and allied factors which are often overlooked in the growth of an art museum.

The artistic content and worth of this museum are properly embodied in the works of art entrusted to its care. For presentation and study of these works the reader is referred to the new edition of the Museum's *Handbook,* its new volume of *Selected Works,* to the Museum *Bulletin,* and to the various catalogues now in press or preparation. Much of this publication program is a special product of our Golden Anniversary year and is made possible by the more than generous grant made by The John Huntington Art and Polytechnic Trust, as well as by monies furnished from the Museum's funds, and in the case of the new collection catalogues, by grants from the Ford Foundation. The sympathy and understanding of Lewis B. Williams, Chairman of the Board of The Huntington Trust, for the Museum and for its expanded publications

vi

program is most gratefully acknowledged with heartfelt thanks. The President of the Museum's Board of Trustees, Mrs. R. Henry Norweb, has been indefatigable in her encouragement of these serious tasks, and without her enthusiastic support, and that of the Trustees of the Museum and those of the Huntington Trust, this program could not have been attempted, much less completed. We are also indebted to Dr. Merald Wrolstad, Editor of Museum Publications, for the final form of this and our other special publications during this fiftieth anniversary year.

Sherman E. Lee

Preface

THIS SHORT HISTORY of The Cleveland Museum of Art
is concerned with the more important events in the life
of an institution which has played a significant role in the cultural progress of a growing and constantly changing metropolitan community during the last fifty years. In that time the
Cleveland Museum also has become one of the leading art
centers of the world. I have avoided loading the narrative
with names and incidents of purely local appeal in the hope
that the story may be of interest and value to the museum
world and the general public.

I can claim no competence as a connoisseur of art, art critic,
or art historian. This book is not concerned primarily with
the enumeration and evaluation of the many important art
objects which the Museum has accumulated, but rather with
Cleveland's experience as part of the social and cultural history of twentieth-century America.

Footnotes have been kept to a minimum. The account is
based mainly on the official minutes of the Board of Trustees,
the monthly *Bulletin* of the Museum, the annual reports of
the directors and the staff, many volumes of newspaper and
periodical material, and voluminous correspondence in the
Museum's files, to all of which the director gave me unrestricted access.

Special thanks go to Dr. Sherman E. Lee for many helpful suggestions and criticisms, and to members of the staff who so willingly provided detailed information about the activities of their respective departments.

C.W.

Cleveland
April 1, 1966

Contents

THE FIRST FIFTY YEARS

CHAPTER ONE

From Village to Metropolis

W HILE I WAS in New Connecticut I laid out a town on the bank of Lake Erie, which was called by my name, and I believe the child is now born that may live to see the place as large as Old Windham [Connecticut]." [1]

This was the cautious prediction of Moses Cleaveland, a Yale graduate and a veteran of the American Revolution, whose surveying party reached the mouth of the Cuyahoga River on July 22, 1796, and laid out a town on its eastern bank. The survey was made for the Connecticut Land Company, in which Cleaveland was a director. The Company had contracted to buy three million acres, for forty cents an acre, in that part of the Western Reserve which Connecticut had reserved in 1786 when it surrendered its western land claims to the federal government, and from which it already had made grants to the victims of destructive British raids into Connecticut during the Revolutionary War. This "New Connecticut" of the Western Reserve comprised roughly 3.5 million acres and extended west from the Pennsylvania line for about 120 miles between Lake Erie and the 41st parallel.

1

Moses Cleaveland's village did not lie along the main route of westward expansion, which still followed the Ohio River as the most practical approach to the Ohio country. Communication with the East was difficult for the little village on the Cuyahoga and opportunities for trade with the hinterland were as yet very few. One of the smallest settlements in the Western Reserve, Cleveland experienced all the problems of survival of a typical frontier community planted in a wilderness and engaged in a primitive agrarian economy. Its population was wholly of New England origin. The War of 1812 provided the first substantial stimulus for trade with the surrounding territory, and before long Cleveland became a port of call for the steamers that began to ply the lake. The village was growing, but progress was disappointingly slow.

Cleaveland, in the best New England tradition, had laid out a ten-acre Public Square. It was to be bisected by two wide streets and divided by other streets into four oblongs, but only a few log cabins marked the village that bore the founder's name. Their hardy occupants had to brave the trials of making a settlement out of a forest, and suffered regularly from that common frontier malady—the ague—whose symptoms were intermittent attacks of chills, fever, and nausea. By 1810 the population numbered 57 souls; by 1815 the village consisted of 34 houses and some 150 inhabitants.

Alfred Kelley probably built the first brick house in the village; David Long, an ancestor of John Long Severance, was its first practicing physician. Crude roads were being built; a stagecoach ran from Cleveland to Pittsburgh and Buffalo. In 1818 the first steamboat on Lake Erie arrived, and the federal government granted $5,000 for harbor improvements. By 1830 the population of Cleveland—"the gem of the west"—numbered 1,075.

The next two decades were a period of mercantile expansion during which many of the foundations of Cleveland's future material prosperity were laid. 1830 to 1850 was the canal period in Ohio's history, and the selection of Cleveland as the northern terminal of the state's meandering canal system, connecting the Ohio River with Lake Erie and fed by numerous branch lines, was the determining factor in the transition of a New England village into a city. The canal made the town a commercial center for western Pennsylvania, central Ohio, and the shores of the Great Lakes. The state's canal system was virtually completed in 1834, and five years later 20,000 passengers arrived in the lake port by canal boat.

Work on the canal began in Cleveland in 1825, with Governor De Witt Clinton, the promoter of the "Big Ditch" (Erie Canal) in New York, the honored guest for the occasion. About 2,000 workmen, some of them Germans but most of them Irish, swarmed into the area to do the digging, at thirty cents a day plus board and jiggers of whiskey, and to fight the mud, the landslides, the mosquitoes, and the fevers that were part of their hazardous jobs. On July 4, 1827, the Western Reserve portion of the canal was formally opened. An official party came down the 37 miles from Akron, in a canal boat called the *State of Ohio*, which had to pass through 41 locks before its passengers could be welcomed in Cleveland with booming cannons, a brass band, and a formal dinner at which 23 toasts were drunk. With the completion of the state system, business flowed into Cleveland and tolls skyrocketed. The trip by canal boat from Portsmouth to the lake terminal could be made in eighty hours.

Although cows still leaned against the fence in Public Square in 1840 and the region east of the Square was largely forest, the canal trade resulted in a notable commercial expansion. Fifty business establishments and forwarding houses, with offices, banks, and warehouses, sprang up along the Cuyahoga River bank and did a flourishing commission busi-

3

ness by exchanging the region's agricultural products for the manufactured goods that came from the East. Population grew apace—10,135 in 1846; 17,834 four years later. In 1854 Ohio City, the community west of the Cuyahoga River, was united with Cleveland into one municipality. The village was becoming a sprawling town. With the expansion of business new residential areas had to be developed to meet the temporary housing shortage and it was during the canal era that the stately homes of brick and mortar, surrounded by lawns and iron fences, began to appear on Euclid Avenue, to make that street one of the most impressive in the country.

Cleveland's prosperity in these years was based on trade, channeled through a steadily growing number of retail and wholesale houses. The bulk of the goods came in by canal and lake boats. Taverns gave way to hotels, but livestock still could be seen on Public Square in the 1850's; and the town badly needed sidewalks, paved streets, sewers, fire protection, street lights, and other improvements necessary for good urban living.

In 1855 not a single passenger arrived in Cleveland by canal boat, for Ohio's canal era was ended, and the railroads, after a bitter struggle with vested canal interests, continued the task of transforming Cleveland into a booming industrial city. In 1851 the Cincinnati, Columbus and Cleveland Railroad, whose president was the same Alfred Kelley who had served so well as Ohio's commissioner of canals, was completed after fifteen years of financial struggle, mergers, and stock deals. The road's first train arrived in Cleveland on February 18, 1851, but the real celebration was postponed until Washington's Birthday, when a special train came in from Columbus drawn by a wood-fired, brass-trimmed locomotive, *The Cleveland,* which brought Governor Reuben Wood to help celebrate the happy occasion. The locomotive had no cowcatcher or headlights, and relied wholly on hand brakes and a shrieking whistle for matters of safety. Amasa Stone had been the building superintendent for the road. When Kelley retired as president in 1853, he was succeeded by Henry B. Payne, another prominent figure in Cleveland's industrial development.

In the first three months the C. C. and C. carried over 30,000 passengers, and in 1852 there were three trains daily between the Ohio River towns and the booming lake port. In 1856 "a lightning train" made the run in eight hours. Other railroads connected Cleveland with East and West, and by the time of the Civil War Ohio's railroad mileage was 2,788 miles. The population of Cleveland reached nearly 93,000 in 1870. Coal was coming in from Pittsburgh and Youngstown, and several companies were beginning to use low-grade iron ore from Ohio for manufacturing. Public Square was changing from a village green to a commercial office center, and the Flats, the area along the Cuyahoga where industry was located, was becoming an industrial slum. In the residential section of Euclid Avenue, on the other hand, Hinman B. Hurlbut, in 1855, built a beautiful home for $13,000; the Rockefeller residence was large and pretentious, and Amasa Stone built a mansion of over 700,000 bricks in 1858 and equipped it with a fireproof furnace, and a hot-water boiler.[2]

Modern Cleveland, as an industrial metropolis, with its nearly fifty different nationality groups, was born when iron ore was discovered in the Mesabi Range on Lake Superior and oil was struck in Titusville, Pennsylvania, although small quantities of iron had been produced in Cleveland during the canal era from coal and ore brought from the interior by canal boats and some Cleveland merchants had invested their surplus capital in Ohio coal mines. A million baskets of coal were consumed for fuel in the city in 1845. William A. Otis had established the first iron works five years earlier, George

W. Worthington produced some bar iron, and Henry Chisholm started an iron business which developed into the Cleveland Rolling Mill.

In 1852 the first small shipment of ore arrived in Cleveland from the Lake Superior region, and the town was on its way to becoming "the Sheffield of America," "smoking itself into prosperity." Cleveland lay between the greatest beds of iron ore in the world and the great soft coal deposits in Pennsylvania. In Cleveland coal and iron could meet, and Cleveland merchants and bankers had the necessary capital to invest in the new processes of converting ore into pig iron, wire, nails, nuts, bolts, malleable castings, and all the other ancillary products of this new age of iron and steel. By 1870 there were fourteen rolling mills in the Cleveland area. Cow pastures gave way to manufacturing plants and oil refineries, and by 1876 Cleveland was half village and half city.

Meantime John D. Rockefeller was building Standard Oil from the "black gold" which spurted from newly-opened oil wells. Born in the Western Reserve, Rockefeller began as a clerk, then went with a partner into the commission business and handled grain and produce. By 1863 he was a member of the firm of Andrews, Clark and Company which was engaged in refining oil. Rockefeller was the genius of the organization, and the Standard Oil Company was incorporated in 1870, swallowed or absorbed its competitors, and built its own pipe lines and cooperage works. Rockefeller became one of the wealthiest men in America and carried many of his associates with him into unexpected affluence.

The Industrial Revolution in iron, coal, and oil burst upon Cleveland during the Civil War and succeeding decades and laid the foundations of an amazing prosperity and a considerable number of private fortunes. This era of unrestricted enterprise, with its cult of uninterrupted progress, spurred generations of Clevelanders into creative activity.

Unfortunately it also sharpened the contrasts between fashionable Cleveland and its poorer parts. There was a vast difference between Millionaire's Row on Euclid Avenue and Dutch Hill or the Triangle in the Flats, where the residents, many of them newly arrived from Europe, lived in the dirt, noise, and smoke in a monotonous row of frame houses so crowded upon each other that there was no room for yards. To the older immigration from Germany and the British Isles now were added the thousands who came from southern and eastern Europe to provide the unskilled labor supply for Cleveland's expanding industry. Before long the city had not only a Dutch Hill, a Wooden Shoe Alley and a Whiskey Island, but several Little Italies, a Cabbage Patch and other enclaves of the newer immigration.

These people came at a time when labor generally was regarded as an expendable commodity to be bought at the lowest competitive price on the labor market. In the 1880's the average annual wage was $350 to $560, and miners in Ohio's coal towns earned $10 a week, with frequent layoffs. Hours were long and wages low. There was no unemployment insurance or workmen's compensation law or social security or any of the other ameliorating devices of the modern "welfare state." It was an age of rugged individualism and *laissez-faire* economics, in which the gospel of rags to riches was buttressed by the philosophy of Social Darwinism. Not unlike many other cities during these years, Cleveland was experiencing the difficult problems of its industrial adolescence.

The first contingent of Poles was brought to Cleveland in boxcars to break a strike in the Newburgh mills. Before long they struck against their employers in a demonstration which threatened to develop into a bloody riot. Strikes and lockouts were frequent in this turbulent period of industrial adjustment as labor struggled for collective bargaining and the recognition of their unions, and employers fought for what

7

they believed was the defense of property rights and law and order. The police and militia frequently were called in to quell the disorders. The membership of Troop A of the Ohio National Guard reflected the struggle that was going on between labor and capital. On its rolls appeared such prominent Cleveland family names as Chisholm, Garretson, Mather, Hickox, Worthington, and others who represented the upper social and economic group in Cleveland society.[3] John Hay's novel, *The Breadwinners,* which ran serially in *Century Magazine* in 1883, dramatized the continuing struggle between capital and labor from the point of view of the defenders of law and order. Martin A. Foran's *The Other Side* was the literary effort of a moderate labor leader who looked beyond "the gilded screen that conceals the dark side of life."

To turn again to the brighter side of the coin, there emerged in this period of turbulent industrial adolescence a number of wealthy Clevelanders who agreed with Andrew Carnegie that the rich should "hold and use wealth in trust for the good of society." From this concept of stewardship resulted the generous support of many of Cleveland's cultural, civic, and charitable institutions. The names of many of these civic-minded Clevelanders will appear in succeeding pages, for without their interest and support The Cleveland Museum of Art could not have been founded. Here it is necessary to name only a few, but the cultural contributions of these captains of business and industry can hardly be overestimated.

The great majority were of old New England stock; there was much intermarriage in the group, and their names appeared in Cleveland's first *Social Directory,* issued in 1885 and since 1888 known as the Blue Book of Cleveland society. Some historians have compared the new industrial class with the medieval kings who also patronized the arts. While their support of culture may have won for the industrial aristocracy

8

a certain social prestige and given them a sense of making material returns to a society which had enabled them to amass their fortunes, many of them were clearly motivated by a deep and sincere sense of civic responsibility and *noblesse oblige.*

A few illustrations will suffice to show the extent to which the cultural progress of Cleveland was based on the profits of business and industry. Henry Chisholm, who arrived in Cleveland from Scotland almost penniless in 1850, founded a company to manufacture railroad rails and bar iron, and was the leader of Cleveland's steel manufacturers. The Hanna family, originally in the grocery business, developed the M. A. Hanna Company, which engaged in mining, the manufacture of iron and steel products, and shipping. William A. Gordon branched out from the dry goods and grocery business into iron mining. Samuel L. Mather pioneered in the development of heavy industry and was the head of Pickands, Mather and Company. William G. Mather, the head of the Cleveland Cliffs Iron Company, could point with pride to more than fifty years of amicable relations between labor and management. William J. Rainey amassed a fortune in coal and coke. His daughter, Mrs. Grace Rainey Rogers, made generous contributions to the Cleveland Museum in memory of her father. William B. Sanders, first president of The Cleveland Museum of Art, was a lawyer, a judge, and an industrialist. David Z. Norton was one of the founders of Oglebay, Norton and Company. Worcester Warner and Ambrose Swasey began making scientific and astronomical instruments, and laid the foundations for the Warner and Swasey Company.

Thomas Burnham, ex-schoolteacher, canal company employee, city councilman, and mayor of Ohio City, became president of the Cleveland Malleable Iron Company in 1874. Charles F. Brush invented the arc light. Liberty Holden, once a schoolteacher, located silver mines in Utah, built furnaces, owned Cleveland's Hotel Hollenden, and bought *The Cleve-*

9

land *Plain Dealer* in 1885. The first Jeptha Wade was a director in some twenty-five business enterprises; his grandson invested heavily in the Cleveland Cliffs Iron Company. John P. Huntington was a shareholder in Standard Oil, and had investments in many other companies. Henry C. Dalton, who left school at sixteen to become a dock worker on Whiskey Island in the Flats, had extensive holdings in iron manufacturing, railroads, shipping, and the Ohio Bell Telephone Company. Charles W. Harkness was an early associate of Rockefeller, and his son, Edward S. Harkness, gave away millions in philanthropy. Francis F. Prentiss was one of the founders of the Cleveland Twist Drill Company. His widow (a Severance) inherited Standard Oil money from her father and made one of the largest bequests to the Art Museum in its history. John L. Severance—a banker and an industrialist in steel, oil, and salt production—built the Arcade, an architectural wonder then and now, and gave large sums (as well as a fine collection) to the Museum of Art, and for the building of Severance Hall, the home of the Cleveland Orchestra. P. J. McMyler, a pioneer in oil refining and one of the founders of the Sun Oil Company, left an estate which his family used to support the Museum's musical activities. The Perry, Payne, Bolton, and Blossom families, among many others, have contributed generously to the support of the Museum.

This is a partial list from among the leaders of Cleveland industry and business whose wealth and public spirit made possible the cultural progress of the city and gave support to so many of its charitable and civic organizations. Their names reappear in succeeding pages, along with many others of equal importance. They had a genuine understanding of what is meant by the stewardship of the wealthy for the common good. *The Boston Transcript,* on February 14, 1925, commented, "There is a wealth of iron and steel in Cleveland, only waiting . . . to be transmitted into the gold of art."[4]

10

CHAPTER TWO

Pioneers of Art in Cleveland

T HROUGHOUT THE nineteenth century Cincinnati was the leading art center in Ohio. As early as the 1850's writers and travelers referred to the "Queen City" as the "Paris of the West," and as late as 1900 its pre-eminence in the art field in Ohio was hardly challenged. More than sixty painters practiced their talents in Cincinnati from 1830 to 1850, and there were between three and four hundred painters doing portraits and landscapes in Ohio before the Civil War. Some were house painters who tried their hand at portrait painting; others, like John Neagle, who did portraits of early Cincinnatians, were artists of genuine merit. One Cincinnati painter did more than a hundred paintings of Niagara Falls and the river, and the portrait painter Joseph O. Eaton was reported to have earned $50,000 in seventeen years of work in the Ohio River city. Advertisements in the local papers announced the arrival of these craftsmen who offered to give lessons to aspiring artists. In 1847 the Western Art Union was founded in Cincinnati. For a five-dollar fee subscribers were entitled to a reproduction of a well-known painting and had the opportunity to win an original by lot.[1]

The decades from 1870 to 1890 have been referred to as Cincinnati's golden age in the field of art. It was then that Frank Duveneck, John Twachtman, Kenyon Cox, and others practiced their profession in the city. Duveneck returned to Cincinnati from Munich in 1888 and remained until his death in 1919. He was an outstanding artist and an inspiring teacher, dean of the Cincinnati Art Academy and a consultant for the city's art museum. The Cincinnati Museum Association was incorporated in 1881, and the museum in Eden Park was dedicated five years later. The Taft Art Gallery, located in the old Martin Baum house built by a civic-minded German immigrant in 1831, was a gift to the city by Charles P. Taft and his wife, and was opened to the public in 1933.

Cleveland, in its early years, experienced that cultural vacuum so characteristic of frontier settlements. Art did not contribute to winning the daily struggle for survival. Few of the pioneers had art objects in their homes; still fewer had inherited family portraits or were able to include them in the impedimenta for their westward journey.

Cleveland art began with the itinerant portrait painters, carvers, and stone cutters who found their way into frontier communities.[2] As early as 1826, a portrait painter advertised in a Cleveland paper his readiness to make banners, signs for taverns, and "other works of pictorial character." Ten years later another offered to teach perspective drawing and painting in six lessons. There were a few exhibitions of paintings in the 1830's in the Court House and in several churches, and in 1840 *The Cleveland Herald* commented that a picture of Adam and Eve, exhibited at the Court House, could be viewed with propriety by both sexes.[3] In 1842 Louis Jacques Daguerre, inventor of the daguerrotype, exhibited French pictures in Cleveland, and two years later there was an exhibition of reproductions of Italian and Flemish paintings.

Occasionally individuals who had secured art objects while traveling abroad exhibited them in Cleveland for a price.

In 1840 *The Cleveland Herald* announced an exhibit of two paintings, *Calvary* and *Christ Rejected,* at the Baptist Church. Practitioners in art advertised their readiness either to paint portraits or to give drawing and painting lessons. A painter of miniatures who claimed to have studied five years in London and two years at the Louvre advertised in *The Cleveland Herald* for January 3, 1842, that "it would be equally agreeable to wait on ladies at their own residences, should they prefer" to have him work there. The next year the *Herald* (September 7, 1843) called attention to *The Raising of Lazarus* (a painting on exhibit at the Court House), explained who the main characters in the picture were, and felt obliged to add that "the man holding his nose is looking down into the sepulcher." In 1845 West's *Death on the Pale Horse* could be viewed at the Baptist Church. The year before, his *Christ Healing the Sick in the Temple,* a huge canvas, was shown at Old Stone Church for an admission fee of 25 cents.

By this time many Clevelanders were apparently doing art work at home, for the papers carried advertisements for paints, brushes, palettes and palette knives, and other essentials. Paintings and art objects were on sale in Cleveland stores; some were sold at auctions, and the newspapers announced the opening of additional studios. As early as 1857 *The City Directory* listed six persons who called themselves professional artists, and there were a number of others who more modestly were described as teachers of art. In 1859 the Cosmopolitan Art Association issued an art journal, priced at three dollars, and every subscriber received a ticket for a drawing of prizes. There also was a short-lived Sketch Club in Cleveland as early as 1860.

In 1865 Brainard's Hall exhibited 64 paintings which illustrated Milton's *Paradise Lost* from the Creation through heaven and hell.[4] The assassination of Lincoln produced many paintings and sketches that were shown in connection with public lectures on Lincoln's career. Caroline L. Ransom, a Cleveland resident, sold four landscapes to Jay Cooke, the Philadelphia financier, painted portraits of Joshua Giddings and General "Pap" Thomas for Congress, and did other portraits of Cleveland notables. W. J. Morgan and Company employed Cleveland artists in its lithographing business, and in 1883 published *The Sketch Book,* which featured etchings by local people. Cleveland families, like the Hurlbuts, the George H. Worthingtons, and the building contractor Colonel Arthur McAllister, were among the early art collectors. That the general level of art appreciation was not yet very high may be judged from an announcement in *The Cleveland Herald* of a picture on exhibit in a local art store, *Getting the Baby to Sleep.* It featured two cats and was described as "a picture of maternal love and kittenly reciprocation."[5]

Although there were a number of artists of repute in Cleveland in the last quarter of the nineteenth century—John Semon, a landscape painter; Louis Loeb, a portrait painter; Max Bohm, who did murals; the Herkomers; and Frederick Carl Gottwald, who taught for over forty years in the Cleveland School of Art—none achieved the popular acclaim, locally and nationally, of Archibald M. Willard, the painter of *The Spirit of '76.* The son of a preacher, and the grandson of one of the Green Mountain Boys of the American Revolution, Willard began his career in Wellington, Ohio, as a wagon painter. From this occupation he branched out into painting landscapes, ships, portraits, and battle scenes of the Civil War, in which he saw service. James F. Ryder, a photographer who used his shop as an exhibition gallery to sell the products of struggling artists, persuaded Willard to move to Cleveland and make chromolithographs for him.

14

In March 1876 Willard's *Yankee Doodle,* later renamed *The Spirit of '76,* appeared in Ryder's show window. Thereupon it was exhibited at the Centennial Exposition in Philadelphia and chromos of the painting were sold for three dollars. The original painting was a canvas eight by ten feet. It was Willard's sole claim to national fame, and the painting went on tour as far as the Pacific Coast. In Boston, its title was changed to *The Spirit of '76.* Later the artist painted several other versions; the original was bought in 1880 for $5,000 by the railroad magnate, General John H. Devereaux. During the Spanish-American War and again in World War I, the painting did patriotic duty as a war poster. On Flag Day 1918 Willard directed a tableau in Cleveland's Wade Park, based on his famous painting. He died in October of that year.[6]

Willard's activities in Cleveland art circles involved more than the patriotic painting for which he is remembered. *The Cleveland Herald* in 1878 reported that the artist had just finished an "enormous allegory," entitled *The Divine Origin of the Flag,* commissioned by Charles E. Latimer, president of the Anti-Metric Society, whose purpose in life was to prove that the Anglo-Saxon system of weights and measures was divinely ordained. Three years earlier Willard had sold two paintings, *Venus* and *The Roman Prisoner,* to a Cleveland dentist for $1,500.[7]

Willard's studio, on the top floor of the City Hall, attracted a number of young artists, many of whom were employed as decorative sign painters. In 1876 they organized an art club known as the Old Bohemians. Willard was its president, and the membership included Herman Herkomer, Louis Loeb, and Max Bohm, and others who became well-known in Cleveland art circles. In 1883 the group published the short-lived *Sketch Book,* which reproduced art work done in the city. Willard's guiding hand appeared in all these activities. His art club developed into an academy of fine arts and into an art school, and in 1893 Willard also was president of the recently organized Brush and Palette Club. When the city in 1898 took over the space in the City Hall which the devotees of art had been permitted to use without charge their art school disappeared. When the Cleveland School of Art was established in 1882, largely through the efforts of prominent Cleveland women, Willard became a member of its faculty.

Interest in the arts was growing and a number of Clevelanders were becoming collectors. Students enrolled at City Hall in the art academy for evening classes and paid five dollars for a year of instruction. The school's equipment consisted of a platform, a few chairs, and some plaster casts. For the Friday night session, the group employed a life model for two or three dollars; on the other evenings members took turns posing in costume. A few classes were available in the daytime for which the instructors fixed their own fees. Membership in the school was open to anyone interested.[8] Among the trustees one finds the names of Willard and J. H. Wade I; the latter was elected president in 1882. Willard was a skillful promoter as well as a painter. In 1877, for example, he took his pupils by steamer on an all-day excursion and picnic to the Black River, where the party could sketch to the accompaniment of a brass band, while Willard drew "comic crayon sketches" for the amusement of the group.[9]

The academy agitated for the inclusion of drawing classes (described in *The Sketch Book* as "the alphabet of a practical education") in the public school curriculum, and when the Board of Education was slow to act, opened its rooms for a night class in mechanical drawing. In its plans for the future the group included raising $100,000 for a museum to be used jointly with Case School of Applied Science and the Western Reserve Historical Society. *The Sketch Book,* founded by the life class of the academy and available for $2.50 a year, actually printed a design for the proposed museum, prepared by Otto

16

S. Ruetenik. The building was to be a hundred by a hundred feet, and would be constructed of brick and stone. As men of wealth were acquiring pictures, "it is an act of vandalism," commented *The Sketch Book*, "to retire a beautiful creation to the privacy of a dimly-lit parlor, where none but the elect may be allowed to see even the uncertain outlines." [10]

Meantime *The Sketch Book* was advertised as a "book of choice quotations from the artist's portfolio" rather than a journal "devoted to the promulgation of aesthetic philosophy." [11] In addition to articles on art and reproductions of the work of local artists, the publication contained biographical sketches of Willard, the etcher Otto H. Bacher, and others, and a description of the process for making lithographs. During its short life *The Sketch Book* was issued by W. J. Morgan and Company, a lithographing firm which employed a number of artists, among them Henry G. Keller and William Sommer.

It is unnecessary to follow the fortunes of the early art clubs, academies, and associations in greater detail, or to chronicle how they merged into each other. Each in its own way pioneered in developing a more intelligent interest in art among Clevelanders. In 1877 a city councilman had opposed admitting the art academy to vacant space in the City Hall, on the ground that "the people have enough fine arts, in fact, making a living is one of the fine arts." [12] Although Cleveland still lagged behind other cities, interest in arts, including music and the theatre, was growing rapidly and there was notable progress in photography, chromolithography, and ceramics as well, and in the art work done in the public schools.

The 1870's marked the beginning of three great American museums—the Boston Museum of Fine Arts, New York's Metropolitan Museum of Art, and the Corcoran Gallery in Washington, which was the gift of the son of an Irish immigrant. Yet writers like William Dean Howells still maintained that the national genius found its greatest expression in "things of iron and steel"; and an English reporter wrote, "The American mechanizes as the old Greeks sculptured and as the Venetians painted."[13] Cleveland newspapers agreed that progress in the arts lagged behind that in industry. Nevertheless, a number of Cleveland families, like the Hurlbuts, Olneys, Holdens, Huntingtons, Worthingtons and Gordons, were assembling private collections of art objects; but there was no museum where they could be shown to their fellow townsmen whose tastes needed elevation.

Times were hard in the 1870's, following the panic of 1873. Cleveland's mayor in 1877 offered to take a cut in his salary, and the Public Library was closed temporarily. Because of the continuing depression a number of prominent Cleveland women hit upon the idea of promoting a loan exhibition of art objects, charging an admission fee of twenty-five cents, and donating the proceeds to the Huron Road and City Hospitals. Among the sponsors of the Exposition of 1878 one finds most of Cleveland's elite—the Hays, Haydens, Eells, Wades, Mathers, Nortons, Severances, Hurlbuts and dozens more. The array of committee members filled five pages of the catalogue, and it required nine pages of double columns to list the patrons.

The exposition was held in an old high-school building downtown. Over 40,000, including 2,100 school children, came to see the displays. The proceeds were $12,880.89. Excursion trains brought visitors from Erie, Toledo, Dayton, and other cities. On opening night, the nineteen-piece Germania Orchestra furnished background music, and various organizations attended in their uniform regalia.

Cultured Clevelanders, the leaders of society, emptied their houses for the occasion. The catalogue listed nearly a score of categories. In ceramics and textiles there were 386 items garnered from all over the world. A room full of bric-a-brac fea-

THE CLEVELAND MUSEUM
OF ART

Founders

John P. Huntington

Presidents

J. H. Wade II,
a Founder of
the Museum (above),
was also its President
from 1920 to 1925

William B. Sanders
1915–1919

John L. Severance
1926–1935

Horace Kelley

Hinman B. Hurlbut

J. H. Wade II

William G. Mather
1936–1949

Harold T. Clark
1950–1962

Mrs. R. Henry Norweb
1962–

A class in music appreciation listening to an organ recital by Douglas
Moore, the Museum's second curator of music, in the early twenties.

tured a cane which Lincon was supposed to have carried on the night of his assassination. There were 320 items under books and manuscripts. There were coin collections, musical instruments, 244 pieces of bronze and statuary, collections of gems and laces, an Oriental collection, and finally 163 oil paintings (of which Mrs. Hurlbut owned 26), and 67 water colors, half of them painted by local artists. The 39 pieces of sculpture included busts of the first two Roman Catholic bishops of Cleveland. The entire third floor of the exhibition, called the home art department, was devoted to the work of Willard and a number of Cleveland amateurs who worked in oil, water color, or crayon. On the second floor the "foreign pictures," sent in for sale and largely from New York, were on display. Amasa Stone bought one for $1,250; Mrs. John Hay paid $300 for another.

In addition to such art objects, there were 521 items classified as "relics," as well as a considerable list of "miscellany." This motley display included a foot stove, Chinese slippers, a sword of Napoleon, a cane from the *Mayflower,* a lunch basket that allegedly belonged to the king of the Sandwich Islands, African nose ornaments, a model of the Erie Canal, a Chinese razor, a walrus tooth, ladies' underwear contributed by the Ursuline Convent, a tomahawk, and dozens of other items. The local papers, especially *The Cleveland Herald,* carried almost daily news stories of the exposition, including critiques of some of its exhibits, and hailed the display as evidence of Clevelanders' intention "to rise on stepping stones of their dead selves to higher things." [14] The *Herald,* moreover, deplored that "such a museum . . . cannot be made permanent in our city." *The Plain Dealer* proudly asserted that the exposition surpassed in quality a similar display in Cincinnati, but one letter writer to the *Herald* pronounced the show an "olla podrida" which "set your teeth on edge and make the cold chills run down your back." [15]

19

It was sixteen years before another exhibition was attempted, this time to raise funds for the relief of the victims of the Panic of 1893. The suggestion for another exhibit came from a meeting of the Citizens' Relief Association. On the committee to plan and finance the undertaking were such prominent Cleveland names as Ranney, Olney, Herrick, Mather, Rockefeller, Holden, Huntington, and Hurlbut. A large hall in the Hickox Building was made available free; the admission charge was fixed at fifty cents, and five dollars for a season ticket. Approximately $10,000 was raised for relief —according to one account, $13,000—and the proceeds were allocated to various groups like "The Floating Bethel" and the Humane Society.

The catalogue for the Loan Exhibition of 1894 reveals the steady growth of art collections in private homes. A list of the contributors included such names as Olney, Holden, Brush, Huntington, Hanna, Wade, and Chisholm. The section devoted to oil paintings claimed originals of Leonardo da Vinci, Tintoretto, Rubens, and Van Dyck, and there were 25 paintings by such local artists as Keller, Willard, Max Bohm, and Gottwald. Over a thousand visitors appeared on opening day. Charles F. Olney directed the exhibition, which was on a distinctly higher artistic plane than the Loan Exposition of 1878, although there were still some bizarre objects on display, including a mummy of a mouse given to a doctor for treating an Egyptian in 1892.

The success of the exhibition must be credited to the Cleveland Art Association. Its constitution, adopted in April 1894, pledged its members to help "develop an active interest in art in our city" and "to cultivate public taste along art lines." Its officers included Charles F. Olney, Hermon Kelley, and Henry C. Ranney; and Liberty Holden was a prominent member. The association granted awards to students in the Cleveland Art School, and its members met monthly to listen to papers and to sponsor lectures "to educate the masses." At the May meeting in 1894, for example, the members listened to several musical numbers and a paper on art works in the Public Library; in June the topic was the proposed Cleveland park and boulevard system, and in November Worcester R. Warner reported on his recent visit to the Metropolitan Museum in New York.

The First Annual Exhibition of the Cleveland Art Association, held from January 22 to February 22, 1895, was the direct outgrowth of the exhibition which Olney had directed so successfully the preceding year. The association by this time had some five hundred members. Half the proceeds of the show were to go to relief and the other half to the activities of the association. The list of committee members reads like a roster of names gleaned from the Blue Book of Cleveland society. The exhibition was held in the Garfield Building, in which the Cowell and Hubbard Company occupied the ground floor. The admission charge was twenty-five cents; school children were admitted for fifteen cents on Saturday. There were special ceremonies for opening night, Napoleonic night, Lincoln night, and Washington night, when the ladies dressed in Martha Washington costumes to serve tea. The catalogue for the exhibit sold for a quarter, and carried advertisements of three art stores, a bank, a carpet cleaning and rug company, and Witch Hazel Jelly, guaranteed "to retain a Youthful Complexion." $9,260 was realized from admissions; $1,100 from the sale of the catalogue; and $464.85 from the cloak room. After deductions for prizes and expenses, the net yield was just under two thousand dollars. A prize-winning oil painting became the property of the association, to "be presented to the art museum soon to be erected." A jury from the East awarded the prizes but the Association reserved to itself "the power of passing upon any nude which may be offered for exhibition."

Besides paintings and art objects entered in competition for awards, the Exhibition of 1895 included a department of Napoleonic material which filled nineteen pages of the catalogue and included such strange items as a pair of stockings which the exiled emperor was said to have worn on St. Helena. There were some rare books on display, and much work from the Cleveland School of Art and the Art Club. There was special emphasis on the work of living American artists, and $1,500 was reserved to buy their products for the still-nonexistent art museum. There were 284 oils and 237 water colors on exhibit, many of them loaned by New Yorkers and Bostonians. Among forty entries in sculpture, six were by Lorado Taft.

There is no way now to judge the merits of these many entries, or the basis on which the jury made its decisions, but the titles of some of the paintings are interesting. There was a *Purity* and a *Repose; Mother and Baby; What Shall the Answer Be; An Unwilling Nurse;* Keller's *The First Thaw,* and a painting entitled *Heaped in the Hollows of the Grave, the Autumn Leaves Lie Dead,* and many others with more conventional titles. Prices ranged from $50 to $5,000. The Cleveland Art Association agreed to buy one picture a year hereafter for presentation to the art museum "soon to be established."

In the fall of 1913 the Cleveland School of Art sponsored a Cleveland Art Loan Exhibition in commemoration of the thirtieth anniversary of the founding of the school. The guarantors again included many of Cleveland's cultural aristocracy, and the exhibits gave gratifying evidence of Cleveland's artistic progress. A number of out-of-town dealers contributed to the exhibit, but most of the exhibition consisted of loans from Cleveland homes, some of which housed private collections of outstanding quality, including modern art and the French impressionists.[16] The exhibition included nearly 150 oil paintings by local artists; eleven pieces of sculpture, some ceramic art, photographs by five Clevelanders, and tapestries, rugs, laces, and Oriental objects.

The Exhibition of 1913 was held in a downtown office building, and the opening night was a gala society event. The exhibit included 27 cases of decorative art. Like the many paintings, they revealed a much greater sophistication in art matters by Clevelanders than the earlier expositions. By this time plans for The Cleveland Museum of Art had reached the building stage. Frederic Allen Whiting had already been appointed as director and Henry W. Kent, assistant secretary of the New York Metropolitan Museum, who was the main consultant in planning the Cleveland Museum, was available to help select art objects and arrange the galleries.

CHAPTER THREE

The Founders

ALTHOUGH A NUMBER of other Clevelanders played an important part in planning and building The Cleveland Museum of Art, the Board of Trustees designated four men as founders, and their names are perpetuated in letters of bronze on one of the Museum walls. They are John P. Huntington, Horace Kelley, Hinman B. Hurlbut, and J. H. Wade. The first three made bequests in their wills, each unknown to the others, for the bulding of a museum; Wade gave the land on which it stands and generously supported the new venture with many art objects and large financial contributions.

Huntington was born in a small cotton milling town in Lancashire, England, in 1832. His father was a schoolteacher. The son took a prominent part in a strike of textile workers and thereafter found it impossible to get employment in his home town. He was married at twenty to a weaver's daughter, and in 1854 he brought his wife and baby to Cleveland, where the baby died within six weeks. In *The City Directory*, Huntington was originally listed as a laborer and "slater," but before long he had his own business and was producing asphalt. In 1865 he built the roof on Cleveland's Union Depot. By 1867 he was a member of a firm engaged in refining oil, and when Clark, Payne and Huntington was absorbed by Rockefeller into Standard Oil, John Huntington received five hundred shares in the new company which started him on the road to becoming one of the wealthiest men in Cleveland. His investments, in addition to oil, eventually included coal, wood, lake shipping, mines in Minnesota and Canada, the Cleveland Stone Company (which worked the sandstone deposits in nearby Amherst and acquired the quarries in Berea), large real estate holdings, and other investments. After the death of his first wife, Huntington married the daughter of a wealthy neighbor of Rockefeller.

Motivated by a deep sense of civic responsibility, Huntington, at the age of thirty, ran for membership in the City Council from the old Sixth Ward and was elected for six two-year terms as a Republican. In City Council he was most active in introducing and supporting ordinances for the improvement of the city—including better sewage facilities; grading, paving, and lighting the streets; and building docks and bridges.

As a practical politician, he sought the endorsement of the Bohemians in his ward, went to the dedication of a new Turner Hall by the Germans, and introduced a resolution in Council calling on the President of the United States to secure the release of Irish-Americans who had been captured when they invaded Canada in a foolhardy scheme to liberate Ireland by attacking England on Canadian soil.[1] Arguing that "the poor man must have his beer," Huntington courageously supported an ordinance permitting the sale of beer and wine on Sundays from 3:00 to 10:00 P.M. In 1866 he was a member of the local committee to welcome President Johnson's party to Cleveland during the latter's ill-fated "swing around the circle" campaign.[2]

26

Huntington's service in the City Council also brought charges of conflict of interest and accusations that he sponsored public improvements only to enhance the value of his properties. His enemies charged that the councilman's firm sold coal, wood, and fire engines to the city. Huntington was chairman of the committee on fire and water. He carefully explained that he had no knowledge of the details of the transactions and got no profit and no commission from them, but the charges along with another that he favored giving a railroad favorable access along the old canal bed to the center of the city were repeated in 1873, when Huntington was defeated for mayor of Cleveland.[3] The causes of his defeat are obscure—but undoubtedly the reaction of the voters against the Republican party because of the corruption and scandals of President Grant's first administration, the exposure of the municipal graft of the Tweed Ring of New York, and the opposition of *The Plain Dealer* played a part in his defeat. Thereafter Huntington became a Democrat and supported Samuel J. Tilden, the party's candidate for President in 1876.[4]

Huntington's interest in art developed late and was largely due to his second wife and a trip abroad to some of the leading art centers of Europe. Huntington had been a stamp collector; now he turned his attention to collecting art objects. When he died in 1893, his will revealed an amazing number of bequests, among which his gifts to develop an art museum were but one phase of his philanthropic activities.

A Huntington Benevolent Trust was created for the support of nineteen charitable institutions—Catholic, Protestant, and Jewish. The list included homes for the aged, orphan asylums, hospitals, free dispensaries, a "wayfarer's lodge" to provide food and work for transients, a children's aid society, and better scientific equipment for Western Reserve University. Every Thanksgiving and Christmas Huntington sent food to a hundred poor families, for he remembered always that he had come to Cleveland "poor and without friends." His will, made in 1889, also created the John Huntington Art and Polytechnic Trust, to provide a "gallery and museum of art" to be open free to all and a "free evening polytechnic school."

The Polytechnic Institute was intended "for deserving persons... unable to acquire a collegiate education." Huntington hoped the museum and the school could be located in one building but did not insist upon it. The Polytechnic Institute was opened in downtown Cleveland and provided instruction to Clevelanders employed in some of the applied arts and allied industrial occupations. In its ninth season (1925) its classes were full, and in 1927 the enrollment reached eight hundred. When the school was finally abandoned because it had served its purpose and other institutions were providing similar instruction, the Huntington Fund for Education, the successor of the Institute, continued to make grants to enable promising students to pursue their education. In 1957 the Fund made 165 grants to students in 35 colleges and universities.[5]

The final settlement of the Huntington estate was delayed until 1928 (partly because of the forgery of Huntington's name by a relative by marriage to a number of notes), but by that time its value had risen to some $25 million, thanks largely to Huntington's stipulation that certain stocks should be held and a part of the returns regularly reinvested. At present, the contribution of the Huntington Fund to the Art Museum's operating fund amounts to $325,000 a year. In addition, there have been many large contributions for specific needs of the Museum, such as major donations toward the construction of the 1958 addition, a new roof for the original building, air conditioning, capital improvements, gallery remodeling, and other projects. The total of these special appropriations from 1931 to 1965 amounted to over $4,396,000.

28

Horace Kelley came of colonial Connecticut stock. He was born in Cleveland in 1819, and left an orphan at the age of four, without brothers or sisters. He was reared in the families of his uncles. Thomas M. Kelley—his guardian in 1837—was a successful businessman, a prominent member of the Whig Party in the 1840's, and the owner of Kelley's Hall in which Jenny Lind, the Swedish Nightingale, sang in 1851. Like so many New Englanders, the Kelleys had made their way to the Western Reserve, where members of the family sold goods shipped from the East and invested their profits in real estate in the growing town.

With his uncles, young Horace settled on Kelley's Island in Lake Erie off Sandusky. He acquired ownership of much of the island, and made a profit from its limestone deposits and from selling wood cut by the crews of lake steamers who needed fuel to fire their boilers. In 1845 Kelley sold his holdings and moved to Cleveland, where he invested his money, some of which he had inherited from his father, in real estate. In 1853 he bought Rattlesnake Island, off Put-in-Bay, and North Bass Island, and sold off the land at a substantial profit. He built several business blocks in Cleveland and dealt in real estate the rest of his life.[6]

Kelley made his first trip abroad for health reasons in 1868. It was then and probably because of the interests of his wife (Fanny Miles of Elyria) that he had his first contact with art museums. Subsequently, he returned to Europe on four occasions. He was a modest and reserved individual, and it came as a surprise when his will, at the time of his death in 1890, revealed he had left about a half million dollars for an art museum. After making bequests to the family, the will provided that the balance of the estate be administered by three trustees who were to acquire land for a gallery of art and erect a fireproof building to be devoted in part to "a school or college for designing, drawing, painting, and other fine arts," and to be open to all the people. The will suggested that the enterprise might be incorporated as the "National Gallery of Fine Arts and College of Instruction of Cleveland, Ohio," and Henry C. Ranney, Alfred S. Kelley, a cousin, and Judge J. M. Jones were designated as trustees.

Among his real-estate holdings, Kelley had property downtown which would be needed by the city to open a street from the Union Depot to Seneca Street. Under the will the city had a time limit in which to refuse the parcel. In the latter event the sum realized from the eventual sale of the property was to be added to the bequest for the museum. Immediately there was a controversy, the newspapers taking sides, between downtown businessmen who wanted the City Council to accept the offer which would free them from any assessment on their property to pay for opening the street and those who wanted the money for the museum. "Let the Museum have all the money," editoralized *The Cleveland Leader and Herald* on December 13, 1890. "There is no city in the United States," added *The Plain Dealer*, "which is so poor in facilities for painting and art as Cleveland." "The point at issue," commented the *Leader and Herald* on January 11, 1891, "lies between the business of possibly one hundred persons and the education, enlightenment, and elevation of unnumbered thousands, now and hereafter." City Council allowed the specified three months for reaching a decision to elapse, and by its failure to act the Kelley grant for a museum profited by a hundred thousand dollars. In 1965 the contribution of the Kelley fund to operating expenses of the Museum was budgeted at $50,000.

Hinman Barret Hurlbut was born on a farm in Vermont in 1819, the son of a veteran of the Revolutionary War. Like so many New England families, some of the Hurlbuts moved westward with the advancing frontier. Young Hurlbut began working at fifteen in a store in Vermont. At age eighteen he came to Cleveland to join a brother already here and to read law. In 1839 he began to practice in Massillon, Ohio, one of the boom towns on the canal between Cleveland and Portsmouth. He married the daughter of an Ohio City carpenter who also was of New England stock. Successful as a lawyer, Hurlbut went into banking. In 1852, while still in his early thirties, he returned to Cleveland to open the banking house of Hurlbut and Company, in which he was associated with Amasa Stone and Stillman Witt. Ten years later Hurlbut had four banks, all of which were converted into national banks in 1863, under the new banking law passed by Congress during the Civil War. Two years later he made his first trip to Europe. In 1881 on his second and last journey abroad he spent considerable time in Italy.

Hurlbut's interests covered a wide range of activities. At his beautiful, spacious home he cultivated flowers and grapes, and he was a prominent member of the Horticulture Society. In 1848 he was a delegate to the Whig convention which nominated Zachary Taylor for President. He was one of the founders of a Protestant City Hospital, where a battle raged between homeopaths and allopaths. Hurlbut repeatedly made up the hospital's operating deficit. He was a trustee of Western Reserve University while it was still located in Hudson, Ohio, and he endowed the University's Hurlbut professorship of chemistry and natural history in 1868. Edward D. Morley held the chair during the years when he collaborated with Albert A. Michelson of Case School of Applied Science in the famous experiment on ether drift, which had a definite relation to Albert Einstein's later theory of relativity.

Hurlbut's interest in an art collection began with his first European journey. He saw Paris under Napoleon III; he visited Vienna and Munich and traveled in Holland and England. He began buying pictures. To the Exposition of 1878, Hurlbut loaned art objects from Italy, France, Germany, and the United States, including a bronze dog imported from France, probably for the lawn of his Euclid Avenue home. In 1882 after his second trip to Europe, the Hurlbut art collection was said to include 58 canvases of which possibly half were the work of American artists.

Hurlbut died in 1884. By the time of his widow's death years later his estate had shrunken to the point where it was too small to build a museum, which had been Hurlbut's original intention. It was agreed by the trustees of his estate that the income should be used to buy paintings and other art objects, and the Hurlbut collection came to the Museum with the right of the trustees to either keep or sell various items at their discretion.[7]

Jeptha H. Wade, who in 1892 gave the land on which the Museum stands as a Christmas gift to the city, was the son and grandson of successful businessmen from whom he inherited great wealth and valuable business experience. The grandfather who gave the 75-acre Wade Park to the city in 1882 had reserved a part of it for the family and a College Reserve; the grandson gave this land for a museum.

The story of the grandfather is a fantastic record of business enterprise and success in an era of unbridled competition. Wade I was born poor in Seneca County, New York, in 1811. His father died when he was eighteen months old. The boy began working as a carpenter, made and played several musical instruments and turned into a "jack of all trades." For a time he worked as an itinerant portrait painter in New York, Michigan, and Louisiana. Then he became interested in telegraphy, and in 1847 he built the first telegraph line west of Buffalo, between Jackson and Detroit, Michigan. In 1852 he moved to Cleveland.

The decade of the 1850's was one of fierce competition among telegraph companies; Wade described it as a "Kilkenny fight" and started to work on the task of consolidating many little lines into a national system. By 1856 with the help of government subsidies, he built lines to and in California. The Indians called the new route "the wire rope express," and it quickly spelled the end of the famous Pony Express. In 1861 Wade exchanged messages with Brigham Young in Utah and in his reply to a telegram from the Mormon leader expressed the hope that "annihilation of time . . . may also tend to annihilate prejudice, cultivate brotherly love . . . and strengthen the Union." By 1866 Wade was president of the Western Union Telegraph Company, which by that time had 3,000 offices and 90,000 miles of wire.

Wade became a director in some 25 companies, banks, railroads, and industrial concerns. A journalist who knew him when he painted portraits in Louisiana wrote, "He is one of those kind of men who deserve to be rich."[8] In Cleveland, Wade served on the commission for public parks, on the sinking fund, the workhouse board, and the National Garfield Monument Association. He built an orphan asylum, served as president of the Homeopathic College of Medicine, and engaged in other civic and charitable enterprises. A rugged individualist who considered himself an agnostic and referred to ministers as "paid middlemen" and "gospel brokers," he nevertheless respected genuine devotion to religion and contributed to the support of two churches which stood at opposite points in the theological spectrum.[9]

The first Jeptha Wade died in 1890; his son Randall had died in 1876, when the grandson was nineteen years old. Jeptha Wade II added to his large inheritance as a business associate of his grandfather the profits that came from investments in ore, shipping, banking, railroads, manufacturing, and the Wade Realty Company, organized in 1910. Deeply committed to the "responsibilities entailed by the possession of great wealth," this "shy benefactor" gave lavishly to hospitals, the Community Fund, educational institutions, or-

33

phanages, and charities for the poor. At the time of his death in 1926 he was president of the Museum, and the entire issue of the Museum *Bulletin* for April of that year was devoted to his benefactions. Besides his gift of the nearly four acres on which the original Museum was built, plus some exchanges with land owned by the city, and a further gift for expansion of the Museum, Wade gave 2,855 items to various departments, an endowment fund of $1,300,000, and other generous contributions for purchases and a building fund. The art objects which he gave the Museum ranged from miniatures to monumental sculpture, from fine furniture, tapestries, and laces to Oriental and classical, medieval and Renaissance art; his paintings included masterpieces from Rubens to Monet, Degas, and Winslow Homer. Wade was one of the incorporators of the Cleveland Museum in 1913, and a trustee of the Huntington, Kelley, and Hurlbut funds. He was one of the personalities that helped make the Cleveland of today, "a rare combination of wealth, leisure, taste, and a high sense of public obligation,"[10] one who regarded the administration of wealth as a public trust.

A gallery view of the first May Show (1919).

A class from Murray Hill School sketching in the Armor Court in 1920.

Over 8,000 people came to view the Guelph Treasure on January 11, 1931, the first day the exhibition was open to the public.

A class from Hudson, Ohio, arriving at the Museum in 1921.

Dedication ceremonies for the Fine Arts Garden in July 1928 included a procession of 28 young women carrying a daisy chain with which they festooned the garden's fountain just before its unveiling.

CHAPTER FOUR

Building the Museum

By 1891 IT WAS becoming public knowledge that three substantial sums had been bequeathed for an art museum in Cleveland. People were already applying to the trustees of the three estates for jobs, from general manager to janitor, and realtors were offering various sites for the building. Common sense dictated that there should be one and not three museums, that it should be financed jointly with Huntington, Kelley, and Hurlbut money, and that it would be well to wait until the grants had grown sufficiently to insure a large and distinguished museum.

A quarter of a century was to elapse before the dream became a reality. Inquiries came from various sources about the reasons for such slow progress in carrying out the wishes of the donors. The Cleveland City Council in 1911 asked the Huntington and Kelley trustees for information about their plans to build a museum and in the same year the Attorney General of the state of Ohio, possibly at the instigation and with the consent of several trustees who wanted action, filed a suit in the Cuyahoga County Court of Common Pleas in which he demanded an accounting from the Kelley trustees and sought to force them to proceed with the establishment of the art gallery and the school called for in Horace Kelley's will.

The defendants in the suit had to explain that changes had occurred in the composition of the board, that it was difficult to sell real-estate holdings while an annuity to Kelley's widow still constituted a lien on the estate, and that the necessity to exchange land in the Wade grant for land that belonged to the city had caused some of the delay. The demurrer pointed out that the income from the Kelley bequest still was inadequate to found either a school or a museum but that plans were being drawn and efforts were being made to get additional funds from the trustees of the other estates interested in the same project.[1]

There also was considerable public discussion about the best location for the proposed museum. Frederic C. Howe, one of Mayor Tom L. Johnson's municipal reformers, objected to building a museum so far removed from the center of the city and wanted it in the heart of downtown Cleveland. Other suggestions dealt with architectural problems and design. Herman N. Matzen, the Cleveland sculptor, proposed a chain of buildings instead of one museum, each building to be historically in harmony with its contents. At one end, on the Wade Park site, he would have a Roman arch, at the other end, a Japanese pagoda. There would be a Greek temple on a hill, a Venetian palace for the Renaissance, a reproduction of the Taj Mahal for India, while a nearby brook could be developed into a miniature Nile.[2]

Fortunately, there was considerable cooperation among the trustees of the three estates. The Kelley trustees appointed a building committee in 1900 and began cooperating with the Huntington interests the next year. For June 16, 1902, there is a statement in the record book of The Cleveland Museum of Art (the name under which the Kelley Fund had been incorporated in 1899) to the effect that "informal discussion" took place "upon the subject of a working union of the Huntington, Hurlbut, and Kelley funds, but no definite action taken." As stated earlier, the Hurlbut estate proved to be inadequate to build and endow even a portion of the projected museum. To further complicate matters, the Wade gift of land had been made to the Kelley trust, thus making it impossible for the Huntington trustees to proceed unless the Kelley interests were willing to lease them the site—an arrangement which was finally made on the basis of a 999-year lease. A building committee representing the three estates had been created in 1905, and as early as 1907 there were joint meetings of the three boards to discuss building plans with a firm of architects.

A number of legal opinions were secured in the meantime. They seemed to agree that the Huntington will was so drawn that a legal union of the three bequests was impossible, since Huntington had specified that the trustees of his fund must in perpetuity retain their power of independent management. On the other hand, it seemed to be agreed that the Huntington trustees could lease land in perpetuity from the Kelley group and build a building which connected with another to be financed by the Kelley interests. Management of the jointly-built structure could in turn be delegated to a new corporation which would act as the agent for the constituent parts.

In working toward this satisfactory but complicated solution a number of the trustees who fortunately were members of the several boards deserve credit for bringing the matter to a final solution. Two, William B. Sanders and Henry C. Ranney, deserve special mention. Judge Sanders was a member of the legal firm of Squire, Sanders and Dempsey and a trustee of both the Huntington and the Kelley estates. He was most active in the consolidation of the three projects for an art museum, prepared the articles of incorporation, was one of the incorporators, and served for seven years as the first president of The Cleveland Museum of Art. The other was Henry Clay Ranney, born in 1829 in Portage County, Ohio, a Civil War veteran, a distinguished corporation lawyer, and a director in a number of banks and business enterprises. A lover of history and literature, a member of the Rowfant Club and president of the Western Reserve Historical Society, his interest in art was awakened, like that of Huntington and Hurlbut, when he made his first trip to Europe, for health reasons, in 1880. He was a trustee of the Huntington, Hurlbut, and Kelley estates, and worked hard to combine these bequests for the support of one distinguished museum.

On July 2, 1913, The Cleveland Museum of Art was officially incorporated. (The Kelley interests had relinquished that title, and were known thereafter as the Horace Kelley Art Foundation.) The articles of incorporation stated that since it was found legally impossible to consolidate the Huntington and Kelley trusts, the trustees are uniting to erect a museum on the Wade land, the "respective parts . . . of said building" to be "owned in severalty by said boards of trustees," but operated "as a unit for museum purposes." The new corporation would operate the Museum "on behalf of said boards of trustees," and accept trusts and gifts hereafter in the name of The Cleveland Museum of Art. The trustees of the new corporation thus became the representatives and managing agents of the two funds, and agreed to counsel regularly with the two boards on Museum matters and to report on the finances of the Museum. The corporation contracted with the two trusts for contributions in the future for maintenance and operation of the building. By agreement the Huntington and Kelley funds would build the building, the former paying seven tenths of the cost and the latter three tenths, and then turn it over to The Cleveland Museum of Art to which all future contributions were to be made.

The agreement was officially consummated January 27, 1914, and signed by eight trustees of the Huntington fund, by Hermon A. Kelley for the Kelley Art Foundation, and by William B. Sanders for the Museum of Art. Two thirds of the original Board of Trustees of the newly incorporated Museum were nominated by the Huntington trustees and one third by the Kelley group. Thereafter, the board of The Cleveland Museum of Art was self-perpetuating. The original trustees of the Museum were Charles W. Bingham, Mariette Huntington, Hermon A. Kelley, Ralph King, John H. Lowman, Samuel Mather, Charles Mather, Charles L. Murphy, D. Z. Norton, William B. Sanders, John L. Severance, J. H. Wade II, and George H. Worthington. Bronze tablets eventually marked the Huntington Galleries at the south door and the Kelley Galleries at the north door but the Museum was operated as a unit from the beginning.

The first joint building committee, with Liberty E. Holden as chairman, had been constituted as early as 1905. An exchange of land with the city, to give a better approach to the Museum and permit the erection of a building on an east-west axis was effected after some delay because the city fathers wanted to impose conditions as to management of the Museum which the Kelley trustees would not accept. Work on the Museum was started on May 20, 1913. Estimated originally to cost a million dollars the figure quickly grew by another quarter million. John D. Rockefeller was approached to make up the loss in Hurlbut money, but declined to contribute. Apparently one reason for his refusal was his belief that the proposed building was larger than Cleveland needed.[3]

The firm of Hubbell and Benes, Cleveland architects who designed St. Luke's Hospital, the Cleveland Institute of Art, and a number of commercial buildings, was selected to draw the plans for a museum and the contract for the building was awarded to the Crowell and Sherman Company on a cost-plus-ten-percent basis. Edmund M. Wheelwright, who had planned the new Boston Museum of Fine Arts, was a consultant and prepared a detailed report on the problems of heating, ventilating, and lighting museums.

Henry Watson Kent, a Bostonian who left library work to join the staff of the Metropolitan Museum of New York in 1905, gave invaluable advice in designing the building and planning the program of the Cleveland Museum. He was familiar with the design and operation of leading museums on the European continent, and he defined the functions of a museum as "acquisition, exhibition, and exposition." He remained with the Metropolitan for 35 years. He created its administrative system, suggested the various classes of memberships, and started publishing a *Bulletin,* first as a quarterly and then as a monthly. He was appointed in 1908 as the Metropolitan's first supervisor of museum instruction and as such began cooperating with New York's public schools and introduced story hours for children in 1915. His influence on the administration and activities of the infant museum in Cleveland can hardly be exaggerated. Kent was offered the post of director of the Cleveland Museum at a salary of $5,000 but decided to remain with the Metropolitan. It was largely on his recommendation that the position was offered to Frederic Allen Whiting.[4]

Needless to say, there were many discussions with architects, advisors and contractors about additions to the original estimates and other problems involved in the erection of such a large and novel structure. In 1908 the children and grandchildren of John Huntington had protested to the trustees of the "John Huntington Museum of Art" when *The Plain Dealer* reported that the building was to be of granite, rather than Amherst sandstone quarried by the Cleveland Stone Company in which Huntington had been a large stockholder.[5] In 1916 the police stopped work on the building on the ground that doors and exits did not conform to the building code, and the contractors were not permitted to proceed until safety director Alfred A. Benesch had been assured that additional exits would be provided.

The Museum, opened to the public in 1916, was one of the largest constructions in Cleveland to that time. The 300-by-120-foot building of white Georgian marble and of distinguished neo-classic design, contained a rotunda, foyers, galleries, an auditorium, lecture rooms, studios, offices, storage vaults, service rooms, a tea room, and a garden court which was an innovation in museum planning and was used in part to exhibit the sculpture of the classical department. Originally the court had cages with birds and a pool stocked with goldfish. In the court was a pavement from a villa of the Caesars, furniture from Pompeii, columns from a Roman temple, Greek and Italian objects, and a Chinese marble Buddha of the sixth century who "sits peacefully in the midst of these classical surroundings." [6]

The Museum was built on an elevation overlooking a pond. Here it sat, stark and box-like, on a recently graded hill full of weeds and underbrush. The approaches to the Museum were not adequately developed until the late 1920's. In 1924 the Garden Club of Cleveland met with trustees of the Museum and representatives of the city government to discuss plans for a more beautiful landscape setting for the new building. The next year the Garden Club staged an Italian street fair in a downtown alley behind the Statler Hotel and with the proceeds employed the Boston firm of Olmsted Brothers to prepare a master plan to beautify the "unkempt and ragged" approaches to the Museum. The result was a landscaping project which included grading, planting trees and shrubs, removing a small island with trees that blocked the vista from Euclid Avenue, making walks and a lake, and adding pieces of sculpture. A terrace was constructed at one end of the esplanade, and on the other end a stone stairway led up to the Museum, which was mirrored in the lake. These plans had the full support of William R. Hopkins, the city manager, and the voters approved a bond issue to finance the city's part of the work. The entire project cost some $400,000, much of it raised from private donations. The result has been to give the Museum, in itself an architectural gem, with its marble facade facing a lake and trees, a beautiful setting perhaps unequaled by any museum in the world. In commemoration of the fiftieth anniversary of Edison's invention of the incandescent lamp the Illuminating Company installed columns in 1928 to floodlight the building.

The dedication of the garden approach to the Museum occurred in July 1928, with a thousand people in attendance. An orchestra played "The Dance of the Hours" from *La Giocanda*, as barefoot maidens in varicolored gowns danced a classic dance on the green. Trumpeters announced the approach of debutantes carrying daisy chains, and the fountains played as donors unveiled the statuary. There were several speeches, and the formal ceremonies, ending with the national anthem, were followed by dancing. *The Cleveland News* reported that from eighty to a hundred policemen were on duty to protect the society women who wore their most elegant jewelry for the occasion.[7] Some months later, freshmen from Western Reserve University, in pajamas, did the "dance of the yearlings" on the Museum grounds and had to be scattered by the police, and on a later occasion, vandals damaged two of the marble benches.[8] Nursemaids now roll their perambulators along the Museum paths, while small boys use the lake for their sailboats, but others have complained that the Museum lake no longer was available for skating, sliding or rowing, or other recreational activities.[10] The area is administered as part of Cleveland's park system, by a commission of three members, two of them appointed by the Museum trustees.

The Cleveland Garden Club, supported in part by an endowment, was located in the Fine Arts Garden. The club has a large membership, sponsors lectures and courses, maintains an information service and a fine horticultural library. In 1930 it sponsored a French street fair in front of the Museum, featuring dancing girls dressed in black taffeta, and a display of Parisians in beach pajamas of many colors, to add to the attractions of the occasion and to raise funds for the educational work of the club.[10] More recently, annual White Elephant Sales have produced sizable sums. On January 12, 1966, Mrs. Harold T. Clark, president of the Garden Club, cut a ribbon and opened to the public a beautiful new Garden Center on East Boulevard north of the Museum of Art, built entirely from private funds, at a cost of well over a million dollars. The new building will enable the center to greatly expand its activities, not only through lectures, exhibits, and flower shows, but also through formal classes for children and adults, on a great variety of subjects related to gardening.

It seemed appropriate to have swans floating gracefully on the Museum lake, and a pair promptly was donated to the Museum. This phase of the plan to beautify the approaches to the building proved most troublesome however. On several occasions the birds wandered far off and had to be brought back by the police. Reporters had a field day, reporting in detail the habits of the swans, connubial and otherwise. When a pair died they were replaced by birds from Holland and named Elsa and Lohengrin. They in turn were succeeded by Philip of Edinburgh and Elizabeth, a pair in which the male proved to be especially unruly. Even though their wings were clipped, the swans continued to walk away. In December 1956 the director of the Museum was sharply criticized for leaving the birds on the ice, and the Animal Protective League sent out a squad to rescue them but without success. Finally, by action of the Board of Trustees, on March 30, 1960, it was decided to replace the swans with ducks and thus protect the Museum and the city from any liability "which might result from aggressive action by the swans."

The director of the Museum began planning the inaugural exhibition two years before the Museum was completed, and a membership campaign produced more than 500 subscriptions before the doors were opened in 1916. The dedication of the Museum occurred on June 6, 1916, and *The Plain Dealer* described the event in ecstatic language on the front page of its issue of June 7. The Whitings headed the receiving line, a string orchestra played, a fountain splashed in the garden court, and more than 2,000 came out for the occasion, the ladies in evening gowns and wearing their best jewelry. At the formal dedication exercises there were speeches by Judge Sanders, who stressed the functions of a museum as an educational agency; by Charles L. Hutchinson of the Art Institute of Chicago, on the democracy of art; and by John K. Vanderlip of the Minneapolis Institute of Art. Henry W. Kent of the Metropolitan emphasized the importance of a museum for all the people and not a privileged few. Speeches by Evans Woollen of the John Herron Art Institute of Indianapolis and Charles B. Sears, president of the Albright Gallery of Buffalo, concluded the formal program. Representatives of forty institutions were present at the dedication ceremonies.

The Plain Dealer hailed the event as the "beginning of an era" in the history of Cleveland. Newton D. Baker had just retired as mayor of the city. During his administration he had supported a municipal symphony orchestra with $10,000 from the city's operating budget, and he hoped that in the near future Cleveland would have a municipal stock company playing in a municipal theatre. The Women's City Club was being organized, the campaign for women's suffrage was in its final stages, Ziegfeld's Follies, with Will Rogers, Bert Williams, and Fanny Brice, were at the Opera House, the Cleveland Orchestra had invited Nikolai Sokoloff as its first full-time conductor, and a Play House Company had been founded to support an "art theatre." *The Boston Herald* of August 27, 1916, ran a long account of the dedication of the new museum under the heading, "Boston has new rival in artistic Cleveland," "the Boston of the Middle West."

The Inaugural Exhibition, which ran from June 7 to September 20, attracted 191,547 visitors, nearly 9,000 on the last day. The attendance at the Museum for the first full year exceeded 376,000. The Museum was no empty shell when its doors were opened to the public. The Inaugural Catalogue, prepared by Hamilton Bell, sold for five dollars and consisted of 360 pages and a hundred illustrations. Among the collections were the Italian paintings which James J. Jarves (first among Americans to collect Italian paintings) had acquired for the Holdens in Italy. There were the Warner and King collections of Oriental art, jewelry and textiles from the Wade collection, the Severance armor collection, other gifts and loans from David Z. Norton and from Mrs. Dudley P. Allen, and art objects from the Huntington and Hurlbut collections.

The future of the Museum obviously depended largely on the plans and the competence of the director. On December 15, 1913, the Board of Trustees had appointed Frederic Allen Whiting at a salary of $6,000 and had appropriated $350 to pay a secretary for six months. The following month, the new director was authorized to rent an office for not more than $60 a month, buy furniture, and employ a secretary for $1,800 a year. Whiting began working in Cleveland when the Museum was nothing more than a piece of land with a fence around it and a hole in the ground. When he left Cleveland in May 1930 to become president of the American Federation of Arts in Washington he had made of the Museum a "human" institution rendering "neighborly service" to all the people in the community.[11]

Whiting came from seventeenth-century Massachusetts lineage although he was born in Tennessee in 1873. He had little formal schooling. He went from grammar school into his father's Boston office and continued studying with private tutors. His only college degree was an honorary Master of Arts conferred by Kenyon College in 1920. For a time Whiting considered entering the ministry. Instead he did social work among the textile workers of Lowell, Massachusetts, and club work with the mill boys. He developed great respect for the skillful craftsman who took pride in his work, and he left a good job in business to promote the Society of Arts and Crafts in Boston, one of whose purposes was to help workmen become more independent. In this connection Whiting learned much about art objects and the best way to display them. He organized and was secretary of the National League of Handicraft Societies and gave talks about the arts and crafts movement as far west as Kansas City, helped establish new units, and published a journal known as *Handicraft*. In 1904 Whiting had charge of the exhibit of handicrafts at the Louisiana Purchase Exposition in St. Louis and served on the jury of awards. Thereafter, he became director of the John Herron Institute of Indianapolis but left after one year for Cleveland.

Whiting was not an artist or an art historian nor had he had any formal training in art education. He approached the problems of the Museum from the point of view of the social worker and was especially interested in children and in making the Museum a service to all elements in the Cleveland community. He hoped ancient textiles would inspire modern designers and he sought to develop the aesthetic consciousness of manufacturers and workmen through the Museum. He hoped the Museum would stimulate the public to demand more beautiful merchandise and the worker to have greater pride in his craftsmanship. He regarded the Museum as a great human document in the long story of the evolution of man from savagery to civilization. Museums were to be "community schools for the soul," laboratories for the development of art appreciation, not simply mausoleums in which to store buried treasures. He wanted the Museum to be a place where everyone was welcome, and where no one looked to see how one was dressed or asked what was his name or with what foreign tongue he spoke. The Museum would be a teaching institution, as well as a storehouse for the preservation of man's artistic heritage.

Whiting's philosophy can best be appreciated by examining his report to the trustees on January 6, 1914. He recommended an exhibition of the work by Ohio artists, with a jury to award prizes, and the Museum to buy some of the best items—a clear forecast of what became the famous annual May Show. He urged a concentration on the art of India in order to give the Museum a degree of specialization. He stressed quality, not quantity, and proposed the organization of "Friends of Art" to provide funds for purchases for the Museum. Above all, he was interested in the educational work of the Museum and advocated lectures, children's classes, and cooperation with schools and colleges. He sponsored a monthly *Bulletin* before the Museum was built, and it has appeared regularly ever since. He promoted a membership campaign and wanted to create an advisory council and visiting committees for the various departments. He advocated the inclusion of music in the program of the Museum and insisted that all the arts should be represented in the temple of the Muses.

Whiting organized departments for photography, building and grounds, and a registrar's office, as well as departments of Oriental, colonial, and decorative arts. J. Arthur MacLean came from the Boston Museum to be curator of the Cleveland institution. Whiting's wife served as the director's assistant, at first on a voluntary basis, then for a modest salary. The new

47

director corresponded with other museum directors to get their advice and suggestions on matters of gifts and purchases and general problems of museum administration.

Anxious to have colonial rooms in Cleveland like those in the New York Metropolitan, the Museum appointed Lawrence Park, a Boston architect and an authority on Gilbert Stuart, to give advice on early American art. The Whiting-Park correspondence contains many detailed descriptions of early American portraits, colonial silver, and colonial houses. Park also contributed occasional articles to the Museum *Bulletin*. Early in 1916 Hamilton Bell, a New York architect and connoisseur of decorative arts, was employed at $500 a month as a general assistant, "to help with the color scheme in the New Museum, and with the Inaugural Exhibition, by getting loans for exhibit and possible acquisitions." Langdon Warner, a fellow for Oriental research at the Fogg Museum, and a lecturer at Harvard, was paid for a time as an expert in Oriental art and served the Museum in that capacity until Howard Hollis came in 1929 as curator of Far Eastern and Near Eastern art. The new curator spoke and read Chinese and had lived for some time in China.

The most voluminous correspondence in the Museum files, however, is that between the director (first Whiting, then his successor William Mathewson Milliken) and Harold Woodbury Parsons. It deals with art objects which Parsons uncovered abroad, and which he recommended to the Museum, with prices, bills, shipments through customs, comments on the ethics and practices of art dealers, the authenticity of art objects, and other related and often unrelated subjects. Some of Parsons' letters were addressed to staff members other than the director and were marked personal, confidential, or not to be filed.

Whiting's contacts with Parsons began in 1914, when the director was eager to develop a classical department. At first

48

Parsons worked on a commission basis; then he was paid an annual retainer, plus a commission and a travel allowance. From 1925 to 1941, when he resigned, Parsons was regarded as a member of the Cleveland staff, and the Museum letterhead carried his name as European representative. After 1941 Parsons continued to write about "finds" he made in European art centers. His recommendations varied in merit but many of the purchases recommended by him and others added to the stature of the Museum in its early years.[12]

CHAPTER FIVE

The May Show

I N THE MUSEUM *Bulletin* for April 1919 there was an announcement of an exhibition to be held the following month of the work of Cleveland artists, and including painting, sculpture, etching, photography, and handicrafts. A jury would award cash prizes. This was the beginning of the May Show, for which the Museum became widely known and which has been held each year to the present time.

The first director recommended such an exhibit in his first report to the trustees. The Expositions of 1878, 1894, 1895, and 1913 stimulated public interest in the community's activities in the field of art, and the Cleveland Society of Artists, the Women's Art Club, and a few smaller groups had sponsored annual exhibitions of their work, but sales were disappointingly few. The Cleveland Art Association, founded in 1915, maintained an arts and crafts shop where art objects were for sale, for the fires of genius would not burn very long without the fuel of financial encouragement. The association probably suggested holding an annual art show by Cleveland artists to Director Whiting. With the exception of a similar

51

show in Chicago, the Cleveland May Show was the pioneer in this country in an effort to encourage the work of local artists through a formal exhibition and to provide a market for the sale of their products.[1]

The catalogue for the first May Show listed a great variety of objects submitted in competition. They included basketry, bead work, decorated porcelain, furniture, including floor lamps and tables, hand weaving, lace, quilts, and woodcarving, in addition to entries in the areas of painting, sculpture, pottery, jewelry, bookbinding, wrought iron, and work by blind craftsmen. Each visitor to the show was allowed to cast a ballot for what he considered "the most beautiful work of art" in the exhibit, and on the basis of this popular referendum, the winner received a prize of $100. William M. Milliken, the young curator of decorative arts, was selected by the director to manage the undertaking and the May Show remained one of Milliken's favorite projects throughout his long tenure as director of the Museum.

At the outset there were no regulations that required the objects submitted in competition for prizes to have been completed within the current year. As a result, early May Shows were heavily weighted on the side of handicrafts, especially embroidered tablecloths, spreads and the like, much of it the work of foreign-born women from Cleveland's many ethnic groups. The third and fourth May Shows contained some remarkable embroidery from the Ukrainian colony in Cleveland, and in 1924 there was an exhibit of needlework by women from the Balkan countries.

Originally each competitor received a personal letter of criticism from the jury. In the first show, contributors were allowed to help hang their pictures, a procedure that resulted in confusion and controversy and was stopped the following year when the Museum staff took complete charge. At the first show, the price range for paintings was from $10 to $125.

A Keller etching sold for $20, a luncheon set made by a blind craftsman for $25, a pair of slipper buckles for $5.50, and a stenciled evening scarf for $15. Total sales at the first May Show amounted to $2,044.50.

Thirty-five cash prizes were awarded, but this practice soon had to be abandoned. For a short time, medals were given instead for outstanding work, then these too were abolished in favor of certificates of merit. Members of the Museum and the Art Association were entitled to a preview of the exhibition and priority in purchases. Each artist was permitted to submit ten entries, and five of the ten could be in the same category. In the case of pottery and enamels, two objects were counted as one entry, and thus a craftsman could enter twenty items. In order to emphasize on canvas the spirit of Cleveland industry, a special prize was awarded for a number of years for an "industrial painting."

For years, and especially during the Great Depression of the 1930's, the making and sale of duplicates was permitted and encouraged. The result was the production of many small art objects, such as pottery, ash trays, small animals, cats, chipmunks, bunnies, and Christmas tree ornaments. One artist was said to have smashed his mold for a cat only when he received his two hundredth order. Such an array of "unlimited" reproductions gave the May Show the appearance of a county fair. The practice reached ridiculous proportions when one artist offered to duplicate one of his paintings eleven times. Quantity and not quality was becoming a criterion of success, and therefore the Museum prohibited the use of the label "unlimited" on art objects on exhibition.

To stimulate purchases during the Depression in a more dignified way a number of Cleveland women organized the Pick-Quick ("Pickles") Club, whose members were permitted to buy May Show exhibits before they were offered to the general public, and who agreed to buy at least one a year. From this activity, the patrons' preview of recent years has developed, and the opening of a May Show has become an important social, as well as artistic, event.

Despite the Depression and the Second World War, the May Show continued to evolve and flourish as an important factor in the cultural life of Cleveland. The public bought in increasing volume, and the artist community continued to grow. The Cleveland School included such well-known painters as Henry G. Keller, William Sommer, Carl Gaertner, Paul B. Travis, Frank N. Wilcox, Clarence H. Carter and others whose work was exhibited not only in Cleveland but as far west as California. Traveling shows, culled from the annual May Shows, were sent around the country from coast to coast, and did much to build the reputation of Cleveland as an art center. Keller's success was so outstanding and continuous that he withdrew from competition in 1927 but continued to exhibit in the show.

From 1919 to 1964 the Museum bought nearly 850 art objects from the May Show for its permanent collections. In 1951 the opening reception for the May Show attracted 6,700 viewers, and 800 objects were sold the first day for $16,387.[2] Since 1919 the show has attracted over two and a half million viewers and has had sales totaling $747,746, from which the Museum collected a commission of ten percent. In 1964 the sale of 300 objects yielded $24,141; the much smaller show of 1965, attended by 77,486 resulted in the purchase of 206 items for $16,201. Since 1939, the prices for all objects have been clearly marked. Various organizations have been encouraged to buy pictures regularly for high schools, club rooms, the City Hall and other public places. Although the average price has been relatively low, some have complained that the artists charged too much, but a proposal to permit prospective buyers to bid for objects in the show was rejected by the Museum as "undignified."[3]

54

It is pointless to cite yearly statistics for attendance and sales. 1927 was a year high in sales; 1935 was a low year. Each figure reflected economic conditions at the time. The number of entries also varied from year to year, as did the percentage of objects selected by the jury for the show. In 1936, for example, there were 3,250 entries by 702 artists; the jury chose 1,059 by 392 artists. Two years later, 3,310 objects were submitted and 901 accepted. In 1953, 756 artists entered 4,242 objects; and 1,308, by 411 artists, were actually put on display. Ten years later the numbers fell to 2,976 items submitted and 896 accepted. The ratio of acceptance of art objects dropped in the 1950's from the usual thirty percent to sixteen percent in 1959, and to ten percent in 1965. In that year, more than 900 artists filed over 2,800 entries, but the work of only 178 was accepted. The drop in the number of water colors has been especially notable. In the categories of photography, textiles, and pottery the jury selections in each group in 1965 exceeded the total for oils, water colors, prints and drawings combined. In 1962 a second jury was appointed to appraise the crafts, and recently an expert in photography has judged the entries in that field. Obviously, competition has become more severe, with a greater emphasis on quality, but even with declining numbers the task of the jurors remains a heavy one, and it is further complicated by the controversy about abstract art.

In recent years emphasis in the May Shows seems to be upon making it a show of more than purely local significance. With the multiplication of art galleries and gift stores in the city, one early reason for the May Show is no longer of such great importance. Cleveland now has a number of channels open to artists who have art objects to display and sell. In 1961 competition in the May Show was extended to include all the counties in the old Western Reserve, thus bringing in such art centers as Akron, Kent, and Oberlin, and making the show more of a professional regional exhibition and less a hobby for amateurs. Because of a sharp drop in art objects selected for display, there were unfounded rumors that the show would be discarded altogether.[4]

Each May Show has required months of preparation by the Museum staff and involved costs ranging from $2,000 to over $6,000. Despite the selection of competent experts for the juries, it was perhaps inevitable that their decisions should provoke bitter attacks by disappointed competitors. Spokesmen for the general public whose tastes disagreed with those of the jury also were quick to give vigorous expression to their dissents. The directors had to bear the brunt of these attacks although they played no part in the jury's decisions and merely nominated jurors for selection by the Board of Trustees.

In the early years of the show, the local press as well as out-of-town papers of importance, like *The New York World, The Boston Transcript,* and *The Christian Science Monitor,* printed laudatory accounts of this unique experiment to encourage the artists of the community and to stimulate its citizens to become art collectors.[5] "The man or woman who makes something beautiful," commented *The Plain Dealer,* "adds to the wealth of his generation in the same manner . . . as one who hammers out articles of commerce."[6] The art of the May Show "speaks for a side of local life too often dimmed by the smoke of industry."[7]

It was not long, however, before the show came under attack. *The Cleveland News Leader* of May 23, 1923, commented on the "incomprehensible choice of uninteresting and even repellent work by the judges," and three years later *The Cleveland News* published an article to the effect that there was no obligation to like ugliness in art or what the artist chooses to call "expressing himself."[8] Others complained that the pictures were hung too high for "bifoculars."

56

In 1930, when the jury was believed to have been quite conservative in its selections, the "radicals" set up a storm of protest. On one occasion Milliken was threatened with mayhem by a disappointed painter, and on another a man had to be restrained from slashing a competitor's picture with a knife. It was true, of course, that juries had only a few moments to appraise each of the hundreds of entries, and there were those who wanted juries abolished altogether and the selections left to the general public.[9] Letters to the editor of *The Cleveland News* charged that juries favored students of the Cleveland Institute of Art.[10] Others maintained that the show had become too large to administer properly.

By the 1950's entries for the May Show revealed a growing trend away from representational and traditional art forms toward what the Museum *Bulletin* described as "the more difficult stylistic tendencies evident in the art of the post-war world,"[11]—in other words, abstract and avant-garde art. Both the local newspapers and some of their readers objected to such insults to "the ordinary decent citizen."[12] One irate citizen vowed he would throw no more coins into the wishing well in the garden court of the Museum, since the money was used for the purchase of "rubbish."[13] Another thought the sculpture in the show had "disintegrated into a sort of supermarket of earthenware pots and amateur welding." A member of the Museum's advisory committee who repeatedly had urged the purchase of modern art and who admitted that the 1959 show was a good one, nevertheless wrote the director to express her "deep disappointment" that the May Show had departed from "old time traditions." The director could only reply that no jury could please everyone.[14]

A letter-writer to *The Cleveland Press*[15] referred to the show of 1962 as "a hodgepodge of freshman paint daubings, framed paint rags, and rusted metal forms that looked better in a scrap heap." A proposal to have two juries, one for abstract

57

and the other for representational art, was rejected by the Museum as impractical.[16] One critic thought it wrong to bring in jurors from New York and Massachusetts to judge an Ohio show. "Better to have finger painting by monkeys," commented another, than the "non-objective daubers" who have taken possession of the May Show with "an adolescent collection of art school horseradish."[17]

In the face of such a barrage of attacks on the Museum's May Show by a vocal minority and in view of the inevitable disappointments that came to unsuccessful competitors it was to be expected that there would be several exhibits of "rejects." "Reject shows" were suggested as early as 1925. In 1928 the Cleveland Society of Artists exhibited "a second run" of some hundred rejected paintings, and this was followed by "a third run" in a downtown restaurant.[18] The financial results of such early exhibitions of the *Salon des Réfusés* were disappointing. In 1931 local artists staged a non-jury show in one of Cleveland's department stores. In 1949 an exhibit of some 1,200 art objects, including the work of fifteen current May Show winners, was held in the downtown Arcade with the financial support of a book dealer, a free-lance writer, and a photographer. The experiment was repeated the following year. Sales on opening day amounted to $469.[19] In 1954 the Cleveland Artists and Crafts Association promoted an outdoor display of "rejects" in the parking lot of a bank, "in the artistic shadow of the Museum," and collected a commission of twenty percent on all sales.[20] To the reject show of 1963 some 800 artists were invited but only 170 responded. The art critic of *The Cleveland Press* concluded that the display completely vindicated the decisions of the May Show jury.[21]

The director also received commendatory letters from people who were satisfied with recent May Shows and believed they should be continued, realizing at the same time however that changes in procedures and content were both inevitable and desirable. Director Sherman E. Lee was quoted in *The Toledo Blade* of May 10, 1959, to the effect that it was time for the May Show "to stop being a bazaar" and to expect more discriminating reactions from artists, critics, and the public. There may be further deviations from the traditional pattern and modifications in the procedures of the jurors who make the selections, as the May Show moves farther from a local institution to one of increasing regional appeal and significance. In 1966 changes in jury procedures and awards of $1,000 in four classes—painting, sculpture, graphic arts, and crafts—helped swell the number of entries and the selections of the jury.

The conflict between older and newer art styles will no doubt continue, and the historian can only await the arbitration of time. Clevelanders continue to manifest a lively interest in their historic May Show, look forward each year to each new exhibition, and appreciate how much this institution, now approaching the half-century mark, has accomplished in elevating the cultural and artistic tastes and standards of the people of the Western Reserve.

CHAPTER SIX

The Department of Education

THE DEPARTMENT of education, now one of the largest and most active in the museum world, was the creation of the first director of the Museum, who outlined the main features of the Museum's educational program. Its basic philosophy and objectives remain much the same today. Whiting's plans illustrate his fundamental concept of the purpose of a museum and his desire to serve the entire community.

In a sense, the educational work is a year older than the Museum itself, for it was in 1915, before the Museum was completed and open to the public, that the director recommended and the trustees approved the appointment of Mrs. Emily Gibson to prepare the public for what the Museum hoped to do for the children of the community. Mrs. Gibson had to work through the schools, for as yet there was no museum. The Cleveland Board of Education assigned a teacher to the Museum whose duties included working with the art directors in the public schools. When the Museum was opened, a Children's Museum, with specimens from the plant and animal world and exhibits illustrating the early ages of

61

man was installed on the ground floor. Whiting hoped this arrangement would be only temporary, for he continued to plead for a separate building to be devoted to the work with children.

Within a year of the opening of the Museum to the public, the Cleveland Art School was bringing some of its sketching classes to the Museum, and evening lectures and gallery talks for adults were an established feature of the Museum's educational program. There were drawing classes for children, Saturday afternoon movies, Sunday afternoon story hours for youngsters while their parents visited the galleries, gallery talks by volunteer docents, and circulating exhibits of Museum materials to schools and libraries. The Cleveland institution was one of the first to permit children to draw in a museum. Visitations by classes from the public schools averaged one a day as early as 1917, when total attendance of adults and children at educational programs reached nearly 17,000. Of this number, 8,434 were pupils who came with their classes to the Museum. By 1919 drawing classes for specially gifted children were added to the program.

In 1921 Rossiter Howard, who had held a similar post with the Minneapolis Institute of Arts, joined the staff of the Museum as curator of education. The June-July number of the *Bulletin* of 1921 contained a special supplement on the aims and principles of the department, in which the new curator summarized its activities. In 1922 28,000 children from the public schools visited the Museum, and pupils from private and parochial schools came also but in much smaller numbers. The schedule for the children of members of the Museum included classes in music, drawing, modeling, and elementary archaeology. Scholarships for specially gifted children for further study in the Institute of Art have been awarded since 1921 on the basis of performance and qualifying examinations.

62

Howard, in addition to his activities as curator of education, also served for six years as curator of classical art and for five years as assistant director. After nine years' service, he resigned to go to Philadelphia as chief of the division of education of the Pennsylvania Museum of Art. His successor in Cleveland was Thomas Munro, who came to the Museum in 1931. The new curator was a disciple of John Dewey at Columbia where he received his doctor's degree. After teaching for six years at Columbia University, Munro became associate educational director of the Barnes Foundation and visiting professor of art at the University of Pennsylvania. From 1927 to 1931 he was professor of philosophy at Rutgers University, where he also had charge of the department of art. In addition to his curatorship in the Cleveland Museum Munro was appointed a full professor in the faculty of Western Reserve University, where he has given graduate courses regularly in his special field of aesthetics.

The general outline of the educational work of the Museum has remained much the same since its inception under Whiting, but with expanding resources and a greatly increased staff it has been possible under Munro's leadership to improve greatly the quality of the work for both children and adults. Offerings have been expanded to include people of college and university levels; closer cooperation has been established with Western Reserve University, Case Institute of Technology, and the Cleveland Institute of Art; and new facilities for a sound and broad program of adult education have been made available.

The objectives remain the same, however. All offerings are nonvocational and are intended primarily to stimulate the cultural life of the community rather than to compete with the professional schools in producing practicing artists or craftsmen. The steadily expanding activities of the department of education have accentuated the gradual shift from the purely custodial function of the Museum to the educational, which among other things seeks to teach men and women how to use their leisure time more profitably. The department has received financial encouragement for its work from the Carnegie Corporation, the Franklin J. Machette Foundation, and the General Education Board. Grants to buy slides, make color prints, and provide other teaching devices for experimental work have come from local sources such as the Cleveland Foundation, the Jewish Welfare Federation, and private clubs, corporations, and individuals.

The department of education considers its program a vital part of general education in the history of the past. In carrying out its function, it uses the galleries of the Museum, lantern slides, phonograph records, classroom instruction, formal lectures, and the pages of the Museum's catalogues and the monthly *Bulletin*. It cooperates with other cultural institutions in furnishing speakers and providing meeting places. By means of circulating exhibits for schools and libraries it brings the Museum to the school.

Circulating exhibits have been the responsibility of a separate extension exhibitions department under Doris Dunlavy since 1960. The collections of this department now consist of some 16,000 art objects from all parts of the world ranging from prehistoric to modern times. All exhibits are designed to fit a specific area or teaching problem and are properly labeled. There may be, for example, exhibits on Minoan and early Greek art to provide visual materials as cultural background for a study unit on *The Odyssey*, or examples of traditional textiles and costuming for a class in sewing. In 1965 the extension exhibitions department served some 140 schools, libraries, and other institutions, with 541 case exhibits and over 800 framed paintings and prints on view. In addition the department maintains three permanent galleries—at Karamu House, the Public Library and the Lakewood Civic Center—

where exhibits are changed every three months. The attendance at these galleries was over 147,000 in 1965, and has been steadily rising.

The Cleveland Board of Education now assigns three teachers to the Museum. They have an office in the building and work with elementary and junior and senior high school pupils. They usually spend half their time with school classes that come to the Museum and the other half in the schoolroom, where they teach with slides and other portable material from the Museum. A number of suburban school systems also send their pupils to the Museum and make annual grants to help finance the Museum's services to their schools. Private and parochial schools are still handicapped by a lack of transportation facilities. School classes may come either for general tours of the Museum or to visit specific galleries where the exhibits can be integrated with the requirements of the school's curriculum.

Classes for children of members and non-members of the Museum account for the major enrollment in the department, and all are free, except for a small fee in a few special cases. Drawing supplies are furnished by the Museum. From the outset, and especially under the maternal direction of Mrs. Louise M. Dunn, who not only managed the details of administration but took a personal interest in individual children, great efforts were made to reach the underprivileged and the children of recently arrived nationality groups. Few children are still brought to the Museum for their Saturday morning classes by liveried chauffeurs in limousines. The vast majority come in their parents' cars, but many still walk considerable distances from the slum areas; some come with empty stomachs and wearing insufficient clothing; some are children of immigrant ditchdiggers and steel-mill workers who come on buses to get their first contact with aesthetics in the drawing classes provided by the Museum.

Children's classes are arranged according to age levels from six to fourteen or over, with special instruction for talented older children selected by their teachers. Nevertheless, art appreciation rather than production remains the major objective. The main purpose is not to produce artists or art historians but rather to provide for children a pleasant recreational activity with youngsters of their own age and with an environment, tools, and materials that will help them to appreciate what a museum has to offer. In particular, children's drawing classes have aimed at developing originality through encouraging the participants to use Museum objects as starting points for imaginative work rather than to copy them exactly.

A lunch hour divides the Saturday morning classes from the free entertainment of the afternoon. The latter may include puppet plays, dance programs, marionettes, shadow plays, music, and films. A Junior Museum is equipped with books, games, and drawing materials. Sunday afternoon story hours permit parents to tour the Museum without distraction. During the summer the department arranges six weeks of outdoor classes in the Fine Arts Garden. The best work of the children is displayed in a corridor of the Museum as well as in the Junior May Show in a downtown department store where prizes are awarded, usually in the form of drawing and painting material. For boys and girls of high-school age who may be interested in the history of art, art education, and a possible career in museum work, a special Museum workshop has been developed recently.

Educational programs for adults received increasing support from Whiting's successors, Milliken and Lee. Regular Friday evening lectures and special programs cover many fields of interest and are intended to appeal to diverse groups. In addition, there are more formal lecture courses open to members of the Museum, and given by competent scholars

66

from the staff of the Museum or by members of the faculty of neighboring institutions. Some carry academic credit at Western Reserve University on payment of the University's tuition fee. In recent years the offerings have included Munro's courses in aesthetics and art criticism; the history of Far Eastern art by Director Lee, who also has the rank of professor in the University, and other historical courses by members of the Museum staff or specialists from college and university faculties. All classes in art history at Western Reserve University and Case Institute of Technology now meet in the Museum and use its galleries, slide collections, and other facilities.

In 1962 the trustees of the Museum established two assistantships in art for graduate students in Western Reserve University with a stipend which now amounts to $2,000 from the Museum and free tuition from the University. Under this arrangement, the assistants work fifteen hours a week for the Museum while pursuing their graduate study at the University. The Museum's Charles F. Schweinfurth scholarship also has been regularly awarded to a promising student in the University's department of architecture. From the outset, there has been similar cooperation between the Museum and the Cleveland Institute of Art. Directors of the Institute, like presidents of Case and Western Reserve, have been members of the Museum's Advisory Council, and members of their faculties have given instruction on occasion in their sister institutions.[1]

The lectures, primarily for adults, have covered the widest variety of subjects. In February 1925 the Irish poet Padraic Colum talked to both children and adult groups on Irish folk ballads. Two years later Professor Michael Rostovtzev of Yale lectured on the artists of ancient Greece. In the spring of 1929 Professor Herbert W. Schneider of Columbia University spoke on art in religion. In 1931 Edward J. Steichen's

67

subject was modern photography, and Frank Lloyd Wright's was modern architecture. The year 1932 produced a series on the life of the first President to commemorate the two hundredth anniversary of the birth of Washington. In 1935 Professor Dayton C. Miller, a Case professor and the owner of a famous collection of flutes, lectured on the history and development of that instrument. During that year the lecture topics ranged from the Mayas and Greeks to machine art and Japanese flowers. Ten years later Dr. W. E. Burghart Du Bois discussed the Negro's contribution to our culture, as part of a Freedom Week observance of Lincoln's birthday. In 1950 the Museum presented a series on Fashions in Living, which dealt with the whole field of interior decoration and design. The following year the Young Ireland Theatre Company of Dublin presented three one-act plays. The programs also have included ceremonial dances of the Far East. In connection with the remarkable exhibit in 1964 of ancient sculpture from India, for example, a Hindu temple dancer presented a number of Indian dances. All programs are free to the public, although the Museum membership generally is admitted before the doors to the auditorium are thrown open to the general public.

Film programs for young and old have been a feature of the Museum's activities, and the Cleveland Museum has pioneered in using the movies as a part of its educational work. In 1939 the curator of education maintained that the most significant development of the year in art was the comic strip and the animated cartoon, which he described as "distinctive American art." In recent years, the films have been selected to satisfy the most catholic tastes. Walt Disney's animated cartoons appeal especially to the young. The film offerings for 1962 included the Marx Brothers in *Duck Soup*, educational films like *The Secrets of the Bee World* and *Underwater World*, and such early masterpieces from the cinema as D. W.

Griffith's *Intolerance* and the Russian film *Potemkin*. In 1963 W. C. Fields and Mae West appeared on the Museum screen for the second time in two years in *My Little Chickadee,* a parody intended to poke fun at the "Westerns." Other offerings in the year's program included *Destry Rides Again,* featuring Marlene Dietrich; *Wagonmaster,* a bit of Mormon history; *The Bicycle Thief* and *My Darling Clementine.* The program for 1964 featured French films of the 1930's and the productions of the famous Japanese director Akira Kurasawa.

Attendance reports for the manifold activities of the department of education continue to soar and necessitate additions to the staff to meet the growing demands for its services. In 1944 the department worked with nearly 43,000 children in the Museum and over 60,000 outside the Museum. Ten years later the figures were 72,302 and 39,829 respectively. In 1964 the number of children met by the staff in the Museum equaled 88,723 and those dealt with outside the Museum totaled 17,449. It should be pointed out—as the above figures indicate—that the emphasis of the department has increasingly been to bring the children into the Museum for first-hand experience with the works of art. The grand total attendance of children and adult groups at all the activities of the department of education, both within and outside the Museum, was 138,254 for 1944; 159,432 in 1954, and 183,985 in 1964. Among the 74,000 adults who came to the Museum in 1964 to participate in its educational program, 44,117 were enrolled for courses of shorter or longer duration; 5,361 came to the lectures, 5,175 to look at the movies and 4,123 to listen to gallery talks. In the same year, nearly 47,000 children in the Museum and 17,449 outside heard talks on art; some 28,000 attended the Saturday morning classes and 7,805 came to the Saturday afternoon entertainments. At present the department of education employs 75 persons, of whom one fifth are full-time members of the staff. The grand total attendance upon all the activities of the department for children and adults was 184,210 in 1965.

During the long tenure of the present curator of education, the department has attracted national and international attention. Munro's definition of the arts embraced music, literature, the theatre, the dance, the film, and the useful industrial arts, as well as the standard visual arts of painting, sculpture, and architecture. As early as 1939 the Progressive Education Association referred to the work in Cleveland as "probably the most active and intelligent educational program of any museum in the country," and the General Education Board was sufficiently impressed to make several grants to aid the "brilliant work" of the department. The board was especially eager to support the development of psychological tests to determine which children in drawing classes should be selected for further training. The experiment finally proved that the best judges of talent were still the teachers who had the immediate personal contact with the work of their pupils.

Although the work of the education department has undoubtedly brought much distinction to the Museum and to its curator, Munro has been perhaps even better known for his prolific scholarly publications in the field of aesthetics.[2] He was the prime mover in founding the American Society for Aesthetics in 1942, served as its president, and was instrumental in organizing international congresses in Athens, Venice, and Amsterdam. The first national convention of the American Society for Aesthetics was held in the Cleveland Museum in 1944. In 1949 Munro was a visiting professor at the Sorbonne, the first American professor to go to France under the newly established Fulbright exchange system for scholars. While abroad he lectured at other French universities and in North Africa and attended the Humanistic Congress in Rome. In 1960 he helped organize the British Society for Aesthetics in London.[3] In 1959 James R. Johnson, an able scholar and teacher in the field of art history, left his position with Western Reserve University to become associate curator of the department of education.

In 1941 the quarterly *Journal of Aesthetics and Art Criticism* was established, and four years later Munro brought its editorial office to the Cleveland Museum, where he edited the *Journal* until his resignation in 1962. Munro continues to serve as a contributing editor and is the honorary president of the Aesthetics Society. From a feeble beginning, the *Journal* of the society has developed into a scholarly publication which now circulates all over the world.

For the non-expert in the field of aesthetics, it is perhaps equally important to emphasize that Munro has an abiding faith that a scientific approach to his special discipline can be found and that art can play an important role in building "a broadly tolerant spirt of world citizenship in cultural realms" and in cultivating a "friendly citizenship" among the many racial and nationality groups that populate the world.[4]

CHAPTER SEVEN

Music in the Museum

FROM 1879 TO 1895 the Germania Orchestra gave concerts at the head of the main staircase in the Pennsylvania Academy of Fine Arts for an admission fee. There were no free Sunday concerts at the Academy until 1917. At the Chicago Institute of Art, beginning in 1911, music-lovers paid ten cents for the privilege of attending orchestra concerts on Sunday afternoons and twenty cents for Sunday evening opera musicals. Music as a free attraction of a museum was a development of the second decade of the twentieth century, and in this field of what has been described as "education in perceptive listening" the Cleveland Museum was a pioneer.[1]

Two years after the opening of the Cleveland Museum, its first director recommended to the Board of Trustees that "the sister art of Music" be included in the Museum's program of activities. The proposal was revolutionary and unprecedented in museum management and it failed to win the unanimous approval of the trustees. Nevertheless, they authorized Whiting to proceed with his plans but not at present as part of the regular budget.

73

The director hoped to make good music available to the masses without charge. He believed the Museum should supplement the musical life of the community by offering concerts that would not be affected by receipts at the box office, and therefore would provide an opportunity to experiment with and exhibit all varieties of music. Once again Whiting was especially interested in the musical education of children which he believed could be accomplished best with group singing and young people's orchestras. He also hoped to attract immigrant groups for community singing, helping them learn English and become Americanized through music.

Education in this sense, rather than by giving music lessons or featuring expert performance, was a prime objective of the department of music in the early years of the Museum. Plans were made to work with the public schools, and Saturday morning singing classes for the children of members of the Museum and lectures on music appreciation were instituted. In 1919 the trustees authorized Whiting to seek funds to support and expand his program and the Director managed to raise $6,000 the first year. His greatest hope, however, was to find someone who would give the Museum an organ and an adequate endowment for its musical work.[2]

In 1920 the trustees learned of a proposal of an anonymous gift of $250,000, one fifth to be spent for the installation of an organ in the Museum and the balance to be applied to an endowment for the music program. The gift was made in memory of P. J. McMyler, Cleveland capitalist and industrialist, by his widow and daughters. McMyler had never played an organ or had one in his home but he had sung in church choirs. The large McMyler organ was built by Ernest M. Skinner of Boston under the supervision of Archibald T. Davison of Harvard. The gift also made it possible for the Museum to acquire a Mason and Hamlin piano and to meet part of the salary of a curator of music.

74

The first curator, appointed in 1921, was Thomas Whitney Surette of Concord, Massachusetts, a well-known teacher, editor, and author who had lectured on music as a social force at the Museum, and who had visited Cleveland periodically since 1918. He conducted "sings" in the evenings for adults and a children's music hour in the afternoons. For the more sophisticated he lectured on counterpoint and music history from Bach to Debussy. Surette also promoted chamber music and some solo recitals and developed a young people's orchestra. His lectures were illustrated by singers and instrumentalists. The major emphasis, however, was on teaching through choral groups.

The McMyler organ, the first in this country to be installed in a museum of art, was dedicated March 4, 1922, when Archibald T. Davison played a recital of organ classics before an audience of 1,200. Unfortunately the organ had been located in a spot near the center of the building and so could not be clearly heard in some of the galleries. This necessitated a second installation, financed in part by the Juilliard Musical Foundation, in a gallery in the garden court of the Museum. In 1933 in a return to the earlier, classical organ design, Walter Holtkamp, well-known Cleveland organ builder, built a *Rück-positiv* division for the McMyler organ and thus provided the tonal resonance needed for the great organ literature of the classical past. It was the first of its kind in this country.[3] In 1946 the organ underwent a general rehabilitation which required fifteen months to complete and which was financed largely with a gift from the Elroy J. Kulas Fund matched by an appropriation by the Board of Trustees. Since the rebuilding of 1946 occasional modifications have been made in the interest of purer and lighter sounds. The Museum organ is the only one Albert Schweitzer asked to see during his one visit in the United States.

Douglas Moore, a young and gifted performer and composer, who had been Surette's assistant, became his successor in 1922. In 1925 Moore resigned to become a member of the music department of Columbia University. He in turn was succeeded by Arthur Quimby, who remained in Cleveland as curator of music and a member of the Western Reserve University faculty until 1941, when he resigned to go to the Connecticut College for Women. Both Moore and Quimby continued to apply Surette's theories of music education but placed greater emphasis on concerts and made greater use of the organ. As early as 1923, the music department began presenting all the string quartets of Beethoven, a series that ran through two years.

In 1942 Quimby was succeeded by Walter Blodgett, the present curator of musical arts. Blodgett was a product of the Oberlin Conservatory, an excellent organist and an experienced choir director. His appointment initiated a sharp change in emphasis of the work of the department, away from lectures and classes and toward more expert musical performances, especially of music not likely to be heard elsewhere and including considerable contemporary music. By this time there were many other facilities for music education in the city schools, the Institute of Music, and elsewhere, and the Museum no longer had to serve as a musical oasis for the Cleveland area.

Largely because of the shrinkage in the return on investments during the Depression of the 1930's, the yield of the McMyler endowment dropped to a point where additional funds were needed if the recital program was to include much more than the curator's own performances on the organ. As early as 1924 the Board of Trustees had approved the organization of a Musical Arts Association to raise money for concerts and other expenses incident to the activities of the Museum's music department, but the effort proved unsuccessful. In 1946, however, the Musart society was organized to provide additional financial support for the department. Members agreed to make annual contributions. Their support, coupled with improvement in the yield of investments and a substantial bequest in memory of a son who was one of the founders of the Musart Society, has given the department financial stability and insured the continued development of its program. The Musart Society's membership probably never has exceeded 150, but the proprietary interest of the contributors has helped greatly to promote a greater interest in the Museum's musical program.

Space does not permit giving more than a few samples of the rich musical fare which the Museum has offered its audiences over the years. It has included Brahms and Beethoven cycles, such seldom-heard compositions as Brahms' sonata for clarinet and piano, or his trio for violin, piano, and French horn, a great deal of chamber music, and song cycles of Brahms, Schubert, Schumann, and Fauré. In 1918 members of the New York Philharmonic Orchestra under the direction of Josef Stransky played in the Museum's garden court. In 1950, for the Bach anniversary, Arthur Loesser presented both books of *The Well-Tempered Clavier,* probably for the first time in the United States; and in 1953 Leopold Stokowski directed a choral concert in the Museum. Two years later there were special programs to commemorate the two hundredth anniversary of the birth of Mozart.

The department has never been especially interested in getting "big names" on its programs and has encouraged young talent as a matter of policy, but such celebrities as Bartók, Ravel, Copeland, and Hindemith have performed in the Museum, frequently combining a lecture with excerpts from their compositions. In the last 25 years, most of the well-known touring quartets and other chamber ensembles have been invited to the Museum. Because of the present curator's special interest in choral work, the department has presented performances of major choral works each year, generally with the assistance of members of the Cleveland Orchestra.

The world's organ virtuosi, such as André Marchal, Jean Langlais and Nadia Boulanger, have been heard on the Mc-Myler organ. The number of Sunday afternoon organ recitals by the curators runs into many hundreds. The first public organ recital occurred in 1922; in 1933, there were 58, attended by over 10,000 listeners. During the first fifteen years of his tenure, the total Sunday recitals and other organ concerts by Blodgett would probably approximate 1,500. The total attendance at all the musical events in 1950 was 23,506. All performances are open and free to the public. In the audience one can find people wearing mink coats and others dressed in lumberjackets; students and old men leaning on canes; children, tourists, and regular concertgoers; native and foreign-born—in short, representations from every element in Cleveland's melting pot.

In 1952 the Kentucky folk singer John Jacob Niles played the dulcimer and sang the music of the Kentucky hills. On another occasion the Museum presented a concert of French Canadian folk songs. Many immigrant groups have performed their native music in the Museum. A Swiss chorus sang German songs in the armor court in 1928, and in the same year the choir of St. Theodosius Church presented a program of Russian songs and the sacred music of the Russian Orthodox Church. The following year featured a whole series comprising the liturgical music of most of the religious denominations of the city. On other occasions audiences were introduced to Rumanian songs and dances; the Ukrainian National Chorus came to the Museum from Cleveland's West Side, and a Jewish Music Festival was part of the musical offerings of 1955.

In music, as in other forms of art, the controversy between the champions of the older classics and the proponents of more modern and contemporary musical idioms, forms, and tonal combinations, has been going on for years—indeed it probably always existed depending on the point in the time scale where the critic decided to take his stand. The Museum's department of music has been criticized for both too many and too few innovations, and sometimes the argument became quite acrimonious.

As early as 1923 Thomas Wilfred, inventor of the Clavilux, "the organ of color," which was manipulated like an organ keyboard but instead of emitting a sound translated music into shifting colors and arabesques, gave "a concert" at the Museum, and hundreds of the curious had to be turned away. The performance was repeated in Public Hall for an audience of 5,000.[4] In 1926, when Howard Hanson's *Lux Aeterna* was performed at the Museum, it was characterized in the press as "about as interesting as the City Directory would be if played by a fire siren, the fog horn, a boiler factory and howling dogs . . . neuroticism in its last estate." The music critics of both *The Plain Dealer* and *The Cleveland Press* were disturbed by Bartók and Ravel's music when it was performed in the Museum series of 1928, and wondered whether the older music would be discarded "as fit only for misguided romanticists."[5] Four year later Hans Barth played a concert in the Museum on a two-keyboard, quarter-tone piano which he had invented.[6]

The present curator has insisted upon the inclusion of at least one substantial contemporary work on every program, unless that program was devoted to a specific purpose which made such procedures inappropriate. As a result, a number of contemporary works have had their first performance in the Cleveland Museum. From this practice the May Festival of Contemporary Music has developed as an annual affair in emulation of the much older May Show; 1966 marks its eighth year.

In April 1959 the department of musical arts announced its plan to stress contemporary music, in cooperation with the Cleveland Orchestra, the Oberlin Conservatory, the Cleveland Institute of Music, the Cleveland Music School Settlement, and Western Reserve University; to this list of participants were added later Case Institute of Technology, the Baldwin-Wallace College Conservatory, the Composers' Guild of the Fortnightly Music Club, the Cleveland Chamber Music Society, and the Musart Society.

Usually there have been from four to six programs each year, the cooperating institutions offering contributions according to their current interests and resources and on a rotating basis. Admission to these "musical festivals" is free. The programs have included works of a few better known composers, such as a piano sonata by the late Arthur Shepherd, a quintet by Herbert Elwell, long-time music critic for *The Plain Dealer*, songs by Carl Buchman, and an operetta.

The attendance is in no way comparable to the crowds that come out to see the annual May Show, but in 1965 the audience for one performance nearly filled Severance Hall. In 1960 the program of the May music festival was expanded to include a "concert" by John Cage, who used tape machines, five radios, a flexible steel spring, and other mechanical devices to produce his sound effects. *The Plain Dealer's* music critic called the performance "elaborate phoniness," was overwhelmed by the noise and left at midpoint in the program. He was promptly rebuked for his intolerance in a letter from one of Cleveland's well-known disc jockeys.[7]

There has been a growing demand for more numbers by local composers on the May festival programs and the suggestion has been made occasionally to adopt the jury procedure to decide whose compositions are worthy of presentation, a proposal which would probably result in reactions similar to those elicited by jury decisions in the May Show.

CHAPTER EIGHT

Collections and Exhibitions

THE RECORDS OF the registrar show that over 40,000 art objects have been accessioned since the Cleveland Museum was founded. The Museum owns far more in certain areas of art than can ever be exhibited, but dealers continue to flood the mail with letters and catalogues about what is still available. The total accessions from gifts, bequests, and purchases for the thirty years from 1930 to 1960 were valued at $18,682,972.50; and the acquisitions for 1962 alone amounted to $1,753,529.99. Nearly half this amount was spent for paintings. The Museum has many fine collections in special fields—such as the Severance art objects that range from porcelain to famous oils; the Wade collection of laces, textiles, medieval art objects, prints, and lithographs; the small but excellent collection of colonial art bought early in the life of the Museum with Huntington money; and smaller collections like the one of pre-Columbian art which is of high quality and represents the whole geographical and chronological field of ancient American art.

Some areas of art have received additional support from

interested and well-organized groups. The Print Club, for example, was founded in 1919, largely through the efforts of Ralph T. King, a wealthy owner of many real estate investments, a devoted trustee of the Museum with a special interest in the graphic arts and the Museum's first curator of prints. Of his total gifts of 870 items to the Museum, 773 were prints.[1] They included one of the finest collections of Whistler prints in the United States. The cast of Rodin's *Thinker* at the main entrance to the Museum overlooking the lagoon is another example of King's many benefactions. It was bought directly from the sculptor himself.

The Print Club was formed to promote interest in this field of art and to procure gifts for the Museum. Its membership included such prominent Cleveland art lovers as William G. Mather, Judge Sanders, Leonard C. Hanna Jr., Ralph M. Coe, Salmon P. Halle, Malcolm McBride, and several hundred others. As early as October 1920 the club appropriated $500 for lectures and an equal amount for the Museum's library with the stipulation that the trustees set aside $1,500 to finance a department of prints. The club's report for 1922 showed that of 299 prints acquired by the Museum in that year, 286 were given by the club or its members. During its first four years the club spent practically all of the $20,000 collected in dues for additions to the Museum's print collection, and on July 6, 1924, *The New York Times* noted the establishment of a permanent print gallery in the Cleveland Museum. By 1932 the collection was approaching 4,000 prints, and it has continued to grow to such proportions that only small selections can be displayed at any one time, although the policy is to rotate the exhibits frequently.[2]

For many centuries textiles and rugs constituted one of the main forms of art, yet they have been perhaps the least studied and appreciated by students of the Middle Ages. The collection in the Cleveland Museum is one of the most formidable in the United States, some of the objects dating from the sixth and seventh centuries. The collection is especially rich in early Spanish fabrics and vestments from the thirteenth century. In 1934 a Textile Arts Club was organized by Gertrude Underhill, then curator of textiles in the Museum, to promote interest in textile art and enlarge the Museum's collection. The club gave fourteen textiles to the Museum in its first year, raising the money in part by the sale of needlework by the members themselves. Dorothy Shepherd, who succeeded to the curatorship upon Gertrude Underhill's retirement in 1947, has continued to direct the club in its efforts to stimulate creative work among Cleveland craftsmen and to cultivate their relations with the textile department of the Museum.

When the Museum opened its doors in 1916, its exhibits consisted largely of loans. In 1963 *Apollo Magazine* of London could devote almost a whole issue to Treasures from Cleveland. Its December issue contained articles on the Museum's collections of ancient, medieval, Oriental and pre-Columbian art, the figurative arts of the West from 1400 to 1800, and other essays which described the tremendous expansion in the holdings of the Cleveland Museum.

As further evidence of the rich treasures which have been accumulated over the years, the growing number of loans approved by the trustees to institutions all over the world should be noted. In 1939, when the number exceeded forty pictures, the curator of paintings and prints, Henry S. Francis, began to have misgivings about the increasing number of loans.[3] He remembered the story of the accident in 1929 when an exhibit of the work of leading American painters was burned in a collision with a freight train near Corning, New York, and all sixty pictures, packed in wooden boxes, were destroyed. To be sure, the artists collected the insurance, but the incident emphasized the risks involved in shipping art objects around the country. Nevertheless the practice has become practically universal in the museum world. In 1946, the Cleveland Museum loaned 48 pictures to 26 different institutions, and the pages of the trustees' minutes recorded the mounting requests to borrow from the Museum's collections. In 1959 loans were made to 73 institutions, and in 1964 339 objects were loaned to institutions in this country and abroad.

The director's annual reports record all major acquisitions in the various departments of the Museum, and by their publication in the *Bulletin* these additions are brought to the attention of art collectors and art historians all over the world. The Museum has consistently followed a policy of seeking quality rather than filling in *lacunae* in its collections and has bought only what it probably would not receive by bequests. Milliken considered the most important acquisitions in the first 35 years of the Museum's history to have been the Guelph Treasure, Filippino Lippi's *The Holy Family with St. Margaret and St. John,* and Watteau's *La Danse dans un Pavillon de Jardin,* which once belonged to Frederick the Great and hung in the palace of Potsdam. It was the gift to the Museum by Commodore Louis D. Beaumont, president of the May Company.

From Cleveland benefactors the Museum has acquired the Holden collection of Italian paintings; the Wade paintings, laces, and other art objects including the Stroganoff ivory, a Byzantine masterpiece acquired in 1925; the King collection of prints; lithographs and drawings from Lewis B. Williams; the Edward B. Greene collection of portrait miniatures; the many gifts from the Hanna Fund; notable collections of furniture, Chinese porcelains, and paintings by Pater, Rembrandt and others, from the Elisabeth Severance Prentiss Fund; furniture, Chinese porcelains, and paintings including Turner's famous *Burning of the Houses of Parliament* from

John L. Severance; the Dorothy Burnham Everett Collection; the James E. Parmelee Collection; the William H. Marlatt bequest for paintings other than by local artists, and many other items too numerous to list in a general history of the Museum.[4]

One way to evaluate the treasures of the Museum and to appreciate the scope of its activities is to note some of the major exhibits of its own possessions and the loans from other institutions which have been annual features of its programs almost from the beginning. These exhibits require months and even years of careful planning by the staff and entail the expenditure of considerable sums. In 1917 the Museum spent $2,111.70 on special exhibitions; in 1963 the amount was just under $40,000. In 1961 the expenditure for a special exhibition, Japanese Decorative Style, amounted to over $10,000. Two years later, the exhibition called Style, Truth and the Portrait cost nearly $14,000; and Neo-classicism: Style and Motif in 1964 involved an expense of $14,704.

Nearly 97,000 visitors came to the Museum to see the exhibit of the famous Guelph Treasure, probably the most widely advertised and the most dramatic incident in the Museum's history of special exhibitions. Nearly 8,200 came on the opening day, and 30,000 in the first week; and it required an hour and a half for the crowd to move in double line past the exhibit. Some came both to see and to worship. The education department discussed the history of the Treasure in 182 talks to 15,000 people, and the acquisition received wide newspaper coverage both here and abroad. The Museum spent nearly $5,000 for special building protection during the exhibition, which ran from January 10 to February 1, 1931. When an electrician in dismantling the exhibit accidently crossed two wires the alarm brought a flying squadron of police who believed the Treasure had been stolen.[5]

The acquisition of the nine objects from this medieval

ecclesiastical treasure—the sacred relics of the Cathedral of St. Blasius of Brunswick, Germany—was made possible by drawing on the Huntington and Wade funds and by gifts from Mrs. Edward B. Greene, Wade's daughter, and Mrs. R. Henry Norweb, granddaughter of Liberty Holden.

The collection included a portable altar, two gold crosses of the Countess Gertrudis of Brunswick, a monstrance with a relic of St. Sebastian, an arm reliquary of silver gilt and enamel, the horn of St. Blasius, a small Christ medallion of the eighth century, the paten of St. Bernward mounted in a Gothic monstrance of a later date (the gable of which was said to contain particles of the True Cross), and a reliquary in the form of a book which told the story of the Marriage at Cana.[6]

These products from Saxon and Rhenish workshops represent some of the best work of German goldsmiths, especially of the eleventh and twelfth centuries, the "golden age" of German art; and to the devout they represent the devotional spirit of the Middle Ages and the history of the medieval church, in all its grandeur and glory in the time of the Crusades. The Treasure had been sent to England during the Napoleonic Wars, to Austria in 1895, and to Switzerland during World War I. When the Duke of Brunswick, son-in-law of the last German Kaiser, offered it for sale through art dealers in Frankfurt-am-Main, the *Frankfurter Zeitung*, the *Deutsche Zeitung* of Berlin, and other leading papers in Germany were horrified that treasures from the time of the Crusades should be permitted to leave the country and pleaded that the remaining pieces might be "rescued" and kept in Germany.[7]

Cleveland's Guelph Treasure immediately raised the reputation of the Museum to a point where it ranked in this area of medieval art with the leading museums of Germany, France, and England. It is no exaggeration to say that no single acquisition in the history of the Cleveland Museum has done more to give it national and international recognition. In the words of the *Bulletin,* it "set the seal upon the future of the Museum as a museum of world importance." It is significant too to point out that the funds for this courageous venture were raised at a time when the United States had entered upon the Great Depression of the 1930's.[8] The cost was $570,000.

Important anniversaries in the history of the Museum have been the occasion for several special exhibits. In 1936 the twentieth anniversary of the opening of the Museum coincided with Cleveland's Great Lakes Exposition, and the exhibition in the Museum was considered the official art exhibit of the exposition. In tribute to Cleveland's Myron T. Herrick, former ambassador to France, the French government sent a Titian and a Raphael from the Louvre; and other loans came from Italy, Germany, the Netherlands, and Great Britain, and from a number of American museums and collectors. The catalogue had nearly 400 entries; 72 were privately owned and 162 were the property of the Museum. Members of the Museum were admitted free to the exhibition; others paid 25 cents. During the exposition, 418,505 persons visited the Museum.[9]

Five years later the Museum observed its Silver Jubilee, and the galleries were arranged to illustrate the growth of the Museum by five-year periods. Over 262,000 attended the 27 special exhibits held during the jubilee year.[10] In 1943 the Museum featured the work of local artists who had been represented in the May Show for the past five years. Paintings and lithographs by Henri Toulouse-Lautrec were part of the exhibits for the Museum's thirty-fifth anniversary.[11]

In the fall of 1933, after great advance publicity by posters and news releases to press and radio, "Whistler's Mother" (*Arrangement in Gray and Black, #1*) arrived from the Chicago World's Fair. The famous painting, said to be insured for a fabulous amount, was transported from the Cleveland railroad depot to the Museum with a police guard of eight motorcycle policemen and two squad cars. Extra guards were provided and special electrical equipment was attached to the frame of the portrait so that any vibration would sound an alarm through the galleries. Great crowds came to see the painting which the French Government had bought for the Louvre in 1891 for $400.[12] In February 1965 the picture again was on display in Cleveland. This time it arrived by train from Cincinnati, without fanfare, and was shown alongside William Merritt Chase's *Portrait of Miss Dora Wheeler,* a gift to the Museum in memory of the Wades. It had been shown in the Paris Salon in 1883, along with Whistler's better-known painting.

In 1936 the Museum presented an exhibition of five centuries of German art, circulated by the Carl Schurz Memorial Foundation of Philadelphia. A much more impressive German exhibition, however, was the display in 1948 of 97 masterpieces from the Kaiser Friedrich Museum of Berlin, a part of the huge cache of art objects found by General Patton's army in a salt mine in which the Nazis had hidden them during World War II. The Hanna Fund underwrote the expenses for the exhibit and an admission fee of 25 cents was charged to raise money for German children. The efforts to attract crowds to the Museum included the distribution of handbills, with reproductions of the masterpieces, slipped under the windshield wipers of automobiles parked at the baseball stadium. A detachment of military police came with the exhibit and had to be billeted in the Museum. Net proceeds from the sale of tickets was close to $19,000.[13]

An exhibition of the work of Gauguin, Matisse, Picasso, and other French "radicals" met with a mixed reception from Clevelanders, and the director had to appeal for "fair play" for the exhibit. Van Gogh exhibitions, in 1936 and 1962, drew large crowds, in part because of the publicity about the artist's private life. The exhibition of 1936 was the first to be subsidized by Leonard C. Hanna, and the sale of Van Gogh reproductions broke all records to that time. The Van Gogh exhibition of 1962, consisting of 142 pieces, toured the United States under the patronage of the Dutch Queen, on loan from Van Gogh's nephew. The Museum had to pay a rental fee of $5,000, and for the first time in thirteen years had to charge an admission fee, ten percent of which went to the foundation established by the nephew to support the Van Gogh collection.[14] In January 1947 the Museum exhibited 87 works by Degas, which were borrowed largely from dealers, print collectors, and museums. Professor George Boas of the Johns Hopkins University came to Cleveland to lecture on Degas and the Naturalistic Movement.[15]

The Cleveland Museum has been a relative newcomer in the field of Oriental art. Its first experience in building a collection proved to be rather unfortunate. Worcester R. Warner, a Cleveland industrialist, gave a considerable sum for purchases of Oriental art shortly after the Museum opened its doors. The donor, however, was not satisfied with the objects acquired, though they were selected by a recognized expert, and he quarreled with the director about how they should be exhibited. The majority of the loans were withdrawn, but after Warner's death his widow returned them to the Museum without restrictions.

Oriental art has received greater attention in recent years with the coming of Sherman Lee, an authority in the field, first as curator of the department and as director of the Museum since 1958, but there had been considerable interest in this field and in the Near East almost from the beginning. As early as 1919 the Museum exhibited objects from the Near East, especially ancient rugs,[16] and in 1923 displayed articles from King Tutankhamen's tomb, to which *The Cleveland News-Leader* devoted a whole page of its rotogravure section under the heading, "From Tut's Home Town." [17] Forty years later the Smithsonian Institute circulated an exhibit of treasures from the same king's tomb. During his tenure as curator of Far Eastern and Near Eastern art, Howard Hollis assembled exhibits of Islamic art, art from Southeast Asia, Persian art, and Chinese ceramics. An exhibition of the art of India was opened officially by Madame Pandit, Indian Ambassador to the United States.

In more recent years, Lee organized an exhibit of Chinese landscape painting (1953). The Year in Review exhibition of 1959 featured nearly one hundred new acquisitions, many of which were in the field of Oriental art. For the exhibition, Japanese Decorative Style, cosponsored with Chicago's Art Institute, Lee prepared a catalogue which reviewed ten centuries of Japanese art history, and the Museum's Junior Council arranged five lectures on the art of Japan. In the fall of 1963 the Museum exhibited Indian miniature paintings.[18] The exhibit of Indian sculpture the following year had been in the planning stage for two years, to say nothing of negotiations with customs and consular offices, problems of insurance, shipping, and uncrating sculpture that weighed well over twenty tons.

In 1932 the Museum exhibited Russian icons from the American Russian Institute. The Swedish government sent an exhibit of Swedish art to commemorate the tercentenary of the founding of New Sweden on the Delaware in the colonial period. A major event of the fall of 1946 was the exhibit of the arts of French Canada. Largely of a religious nature and assembled from convents and churches, the objects included wood carvings, silver, and sculpture from the time of Louis XV.[19] Specimens of Negro sculpture came as a gift to the Museum in 1931 from the African Art Sponsors Fund. Two years earlier the Museum had sponsored the first exhibition of the primitive Negro art of Africa. A similar exhibit was presented in 1935. In 1928 the Negroes of Cleveland raised $1,500 to be sent to Paul B. Travis, the Cleveland painter who was traveling and painting in Africa, to buy African art objects and ethnological material for the Museum. In 1946 the Museum displayed Portraits of Distinguished Negro Citizens, a collection circulated by the Harmon Foundation of New York.

As late as 1900 Cleveland had a foreign-born population of nearly 240,000 in a total population of 796,841. Many strange tongues still are heard on its old New England streets. Among visitors to the Museum one can identify heavily mustached newcomers from southern, central, and eastern Europe, and their women, often with babies in arms, with their heads covered with picturesque shawls of beautiful oriental coloring.

The presence of so many nationality groups in the Cleveland melting pot was reflected in a number of the Museum's exhibits of the arts and crafts of the immigrants. In its earlier years, it was part of the objective of the Museum to instill pride in the culture of the newcomer's homeland and to teach tolerance for the culture of others who also were part of the great process of the amalgamation of cultural diversity into political unity in the United States. For this undertaking, the Museum received considerable publicity in th city's foreign-language press. The Hungarian *Szabadsag*, the German *Wächter und Anzeiger*, the Italian *La Voce del Populo Italiano*, *The Jewish World* (in Hebrew), and *The Polish News*, among others, wrote appreciatively of the Museum and urged their readers to visit it frequently and give it their support.[20]

In 1922 the Museum exhibited a collection of Czech prints. In 1936 it had a display of Czechoslovakian arts and crafts. Hungarian prints were featured in 1925, and on several occasions the local Hungarian community presented books and prints to the Museum. In 1925 Whiting and Milliken addressed two thousand Yugoslavs in Slovenian Hall where the honored guest was the prominent sculptor, Ivan Mestrovic. In 1928 some 400 Danes came to the Museum to see a Danish National Exhibition. There were speeches and songs in Danish, and it was proposed to raise money to buy one object in the exhibit and present it to the Museum.[21] In the same year Rabbi Barnett R. Brickner made the opening speech for an exhibit from the Jewish Children's Art School of Boston. Five years later, the Poles came to a Polish Night, sponsored by the Museum's education department, which had planned an exhibit of prints by Polish artists. The occasion also honored Artur Rodzinski, the new conductor of the Cleveland Orchestra, and the editors of Cleveland's two Polish papers were among the speakers for the occasion.[22] In 1950 in connection with festivities to commemorate the Polish Constitution of 1791 and Polish independence, small Polish flags were attached to the forty-five compositions by Polish artists in the May Show.[23] A request for the use of a gallery of the Museum to exhibit Polish paintings, coins, and medals had to be refused, however, lest it set a precedent for other nationality groups. In 1951 members of seven Irish-American societies came to the Museum in a body to view an Irish art exhibit from Dublin by postwar Irish artists.[24]

In the hundreds of special exhibits sponsored by the Museum in the fifty years of its existence, the directors have not been unmindful of the just claims of native Clevelanders. In 1926 there were memorial exhibitions of the many gifts of Wade and King to the Museum. In 1946 the Museum displayed 28 pieces of sculpture by the late Max Kalish and 26 paintings and drawings by Alexander Warshawsky, both of whom had received their first instruction in art in the Cleveland Art School. The Henry G. Keller memorial exhibition of 1950 was sponsored jointly by the Museum and the Institute of Art, where Keller began teaching in 1902. 2,300 people attended the preview of the work of the artist who had been a major force in the flowering of art in Cleveland. The memorial exhibition for William Sommer, son of German immigrants, apprenticed as a lithographer, and regarded as an ultramodern painter in the 1920's, occurred the same year and included about 200 paintings. In 1953 the Carl Gaertner memorial exhibit again was a joint undertaking with the Institute of Art, where Gaertner had been a faculty member.

The foregoing accounts of special exhibits provide merely a sampling of the scope of the Museum's interests in the whole wide area of art and art history. Theodore Sizer, curator of Oriental art until he left for Yale in 1927, called attention to a hitherto-neglected field by installing an exhibit of pre-Columbian art in the foyer of the Museum. In 1929 a new department of primitive art was established, with Charles F. Ramus as the assistant in charge, and concentrating on the art of Central and South America. There has been an exhibition of gold to show how this precious metal was used by goldsmiths through the ages, of medieval missals, modern architectural models, design in advertising art, The Family of Man in 1956 (with some 500 photographs from 68 countries, assembled by Edward Steichen and recognized as the greatest photographic exhibition of all time), industrial machine arts, antique watches, art for children, the originals of cartoons, the fashion plates from *Godey's Lady's Book,* eating implements which illustrated man's progress in table manners, textile shows, portraits from 1525 to 1872, lithography, the art and archaeology of Vietnam, British gold coins from 50 B.C. to the present from the collection of Mrs. Norweb, and many other miscellaneous exhibits which once would not have been considered within the proper limits of a museum's function.

It is the custom to open major special exhibits with a director's preview dinner or reception for the trustees, art lovers, friends of the Museum, and representatives of the press.

93

CHAPTER NINE

Museum Management

LEGALLY THE MANAGEMENT of the Cleveland Museum is vested in a self-perpetuating Board of Trustees, currently consisting of fourteen members. The trustees approve the annual budgets, appointments to the staff, the acquisition of art objects and loans to other institutions, allocate funds to the various departments, grant leaves of absence for travel and study, deal with wills, bequests, and investments, provide insurance for the Museum's treasures, determine the labor, pension and retirement policy for employees, and deal with all the many problems that arise in administering an institution whose assets make it one of the world's wealthiest museums.

The board functions mainly through three major committees—executive, finance, and accessions. For many of its decisions the trustees obviously must rely on the expert recommendations of the director and his staff. A major reason for the remarkably rapid growth of the Museum is the excellent liaison that has existed between trustees and director, and a clear understanding of the areas in which each must exercise primary responsibility.

In its fifty years the Museum has had six presidents. Judge Sanders, one of the original incorporators of The Cleveland Museum of Art in 1913, was the first. He served from 1915 to 1919, and was succeeded in turn by J. H. Wade II (1920-1925), John L. Severance (1926-1935), and William G. Mather (1936-1949), all of them collectors of art works and generous supporters of the Museum. The contributions of Wade and Severance have figured largely in earlier chapters. Mather became a trustee in 1919. When he retired from the presidency in 1949, he was given the title of trustee emeritus and honorary president. He died in 1951.

Harold T. Clark, the transplanted New Englander who was a catalyst for so many charitable, cultural, and civic enterprises of the Cleveland community, was elected to the board in 1929 to succeed Judge Sanders and followed Mather in the presidency in 1950. In 1938 he was formally appointed as attorney for the Museum although his counsel had been sought on many occasions before that time. He was especially interested in the educational work of the Museum. As a trustee of the Huntington, Kelley, and Hurlbut funds, he was extremely helpful to the Museum. On the death of Leonard C. Hanna Jr., Clark also became the executor of the huge bequest which has done so much to insure the future of the Museum. In 1962 Clark resigned as president but continued as chairman of the Board of Trustees until his death in 1965. He was succeeded in the presidency by Mrs. R. Henry Norweb, the first woman to occupy that post. The granddaughter of Liberty Holden and the wife of a career diplomat whose assignments took them to many countries, Mrs. Norweb has been especially interested in building the Museum's excellent collection of pre-Columbian art.

By 1962 the assets available for the support of the Museum exceeded a hundred million dollars. Thirty years earlier they were less than a tenth of that amount.[1] When the Museum was opened in 1916, the operating budget amounted to $57,-355.19; in 1965 it was thirty times that figure. By action of the Board admission to the Museum has been free for the last 25 years.

The Advisory Council to the Board of Trustees consists of prominent citizens with a special interest in the Museum. It was organized in 1914, when it consisted of nineteen members plus the presidents of Case School of Applied Science and Western Reserve University. The number gradually grew to 41 to be reduced again in 1963 to 26. The council meets with the trustees at least once a year to hear discussions of the Museum's activities and to offer comments and suggestions but it has neither legislative nor executive powers and perhaps might more appropriately be called "Friends of the Museum."

In 1941 a group of some forty younger women eager to serve the Museum organized a Junior Council, with Mrs. Robert M. Hornung as the first chairman. The council has sponsored a variety of activities to promote interest in the Museum and to raise funds for its support. Applicants for membership in the council now must take an orientation course to acquaint them with the program and resources of the Museum. In addition to its full-fledged members the council has enlisted the help of volunteers who work on various projects, including clerical help.

Each year since 1941 the Junior Council, in collaboration with a local newspaper, has sponsored a community "sing" of Christmas carols in the rotunda and armor court of the Museum, which are decorated for the occasion with greenery and candlelight. More than 4,000 participate annually in this pre-Christmas celebration. In 1946, in cooperation with *The Cleveland News*, the council promoted a quiz program, with prizes for adults and children who best identified 44 pictures from the Museum's collection.[2] From time to time, the council has sold tickets for lecture series such as The Taste of Our

97

Time (1959), Paths of Abstract Art (1960) and The Classical Tradition (1964).

In 1953 the council, together with the Near East College Association, staged a Mediterranean street fair on the lawn of the Museum to raise money for the Museum's educational programs for children, and two years later it contributed nearly $24,000 to the building fund by selling "gold bricks" for $5.00 at a Mid-European street fair in front of the Museum. Representatives of twelve of Cleveland's nationality groups participated by offering their native foods for sale and by performing the folk dances of their homeland.[3] In 1960 the Junior Council sponsored a two-day children's fair, with booths, a bandstand, a pony, stagecoach, and small animals, to raise money for the education department of the Museum. The most recent activity of the council has been the Art Cart Project, in which members show and describe selected reproductions to hospital patients, who can choose one to hang in their rooms to break the monotony of blank hospital walls.

The Museum has had three directors since 1913. The lasting contributions to the basic programs of the Museum by Frederic Allen Whiting, its first director, have been described in earlier chapters. Whiting's period of service ran from December 15, 1913, to May 1, 1930, when he resigned to go to Washington as president of the American Federation of Arts. On May 22, 1930, the trustees elected Whiting an honorary fellow of the Museum and designated Rossiter Howard as acting director. A special committee, consisting of Mather, Greene, Coe, and Leonard Hanna was appointed to find a new director. The choice fell upon William Mathewson Milliken, who was appointed director in August 1930 and served in that office until his retirement in 1958.

Milliken was a Princeton graduate. He had been an assistant curator of decorative arts at the Metropolitan Museum before World War I, but when he returned to New York from his

98

Madame Vijaya
Lakshmi Pandit,
Indian ambassador,
at the opening of
the 1949 exhibition
of Indian art.

Albert Schweitzer
and organ builder
Walter Holtkamp
at the McMyler organ,
July 1949.

The Garden Court.

Leonard C. Hanna Jr.
laying the cornerstone
in 1956 for the new wing
of the Museum,
completed (below)
in 1958.

Prospective purchasers line up in the Armor Court at the Patrons Preview of the 1956 May Show.

overseas service he found his name on the honor roll of the Museum but no job. His application for a position with the Cleveland Museum was successful and he was appointed curator of decorative arts with the expectation that he would concentrate on modern art.[4] Actually, the medieval collection and the May Show were his greatest achievements.[5]

Milliken served the Museum for 39 years and two months, 28 years as director. In that time the Cleveland Museum became nationally and internationally famous. The director was an expert showman and promoter; he had courage and imagination to plan a great future for the Museum, but above all he was a man of boundless enthusiasm with an extraordinary gift to communicate his enthusiasms to others and persuade them to support his recommendations. His achievements have been recognized by the award of seven honorary degrees, decorations from five foreign nations, election to the American Academy of Arts and Sciences, honorary membership in the German National Museum in appreciation of his work in building an outstanding collection of German art in the United States, and election to the editorial board of several European art journals. Since his retirement, Milliken has served as advisor to several museums and the Seattle World's Fair of 1962, and as architectural consultant for the National Gallery in Melbourne, Australia.[6]

Sherman Emery Lee, the present director, has his A.B. and M.A. degrees from American University, where his major interest was history, and his PH.D. from Western Reserve University where he wrote a doctoral dissertation entitled "A Critical Survey of American Water Color Painting." His specialty, however, is Oriental art, and three of his major publications are in this field. Lee's professional career began in Detroit in 1941, where he had the title of curator of Far Eastern art at the Institute of Art from 1941 to 1947. World War II took him to the Far East with the armed forces. There he became an advisor on art collections and later served as the officer in charge of the arts and monuments division of American General Headquarters in Tokyo. In 1952 he left his position as associate director of the art museum in Seattle to become curator of Oriental art in Cleveland. In addition to his specialty he was expected to take charge of the Museum's collections of classical and Egyptian art as well.

A productive scholar in the field of Oriental art, Lee, as director, has put major emphasis on encouraging the scholarly standards of the work done in the Cleveland Museum. He has the status of full professor at Western Reserve University and he has lectured on his specialty at Harvard and other leading American universities and in Oxford, England. His rare combination of sound scholarship and administrative talent led the trustees to appoint him as associate director in 1956 and to make him the liaison officer between architects, contractors, trustees, and staff during the construction of the new wing of the Museum. In that capacity he planned and supervised the evacuation and redistribution of exhibits and service quarters from the old to the new building. On June 27, 1957, he was appointed director of the Museum and he officially assumed his new duties in April 1958.

The number of curators and their assignments to special areas have varied over the years as the Museum has developed the several fields of art and as it became necessary to increase its personnel. Munro, curator of education, and Francis, curator of paintings and prints, are the veterans of the curatorial staff, each with a record of more than thirty years of distinguished service in their special fields. The most recent appointment was that of the Egyptologist, John D. Cooney, who left the Brooklyn Museum in 1964 to become curator of Egyptian and classical art in Cleveland.

In an institution like The Cleveland Museum of Art, which is privately supported, the department in charge of memberships becomes especially important not only for financial reasons but also as a means of acquainting the local constituency with the work of the Museum. In 1915, in advance of the opening of the Museum, a man was imported from Chicago to conduct a membership campaign on a commission basis. He guaranteed an enrollment of 3,000 by September 1916.[7] The experiment was not successful, and ever since the Museum has maintained its own membership department.

In the 1920's and 1930's Ihna Thayer Frary, better known for his writings on early Ohio houses and his book, *Thomas Jefferson, the Architect and Builder,* served as the secretary for membership and publicity. In 1947 the Trustees, by constitutional amendment, created various classes of memberships—four groups of benefactors, their gifts ranging from $25,000 to $500,000; four groups of fellows with contributions from $100 annually to $10,000; two classes of life memberships; sustaining members who pay $25 a year; and annual memberships at $10.[8]

In 1916, the opening year, the Museum had 530 members. By 1926 the total had increased nearly tenfold. There was a shrinkage in the Depression of the 1930's, and no substantial recovery until after World War II. In 1954 the membership department was reorganized and four solicitors were added. In 1965 the total memberships reached 9,567, of whom 8,006 were annual members, 719 life members, 46 fellows, and 385 sustaining members. Total receipts from all classes equaled $155,621 in 1965.

The primary function of the public relations department, now headed by Richard Burton, is to secure more financial support for the Museum and to make it better known. As such it publicizes special events, provides information to the press and other media, furnishes cuts of the Museum's possessions, and in other ways seeks to keep the Museum in the eye of the public and the museum world. In 1958, a year which featured the opening of the new wing of the Museum and the Leonard C. Hanna Jr. Bequest, the department was responsible for 1,530 news stories in 126 newspapers and 22 leading national magazines and local publications, and sent out 77 releases. 400,000 brochures were circulated through the Cleveland Transit System, and 1,500 posters were distributed. In 1960 the Museum was the major topic of 544 articles and was mentioned in 1,118 other publications in this country and abroad. The major news stories for 1964 totaled 431.

The library of the Museum, widely used today by undergraduate and graduate students of neighboring institutions as well as by the Museum staff and by visiting scholars in many areas of art history, was opened in 1916 with 600 books and pamphlets, most of them gifts. Over 14,600 readers used the reference service of the library in 1965. The first director of the Museum clearly understood the need for a good library and began early to divert small gifts to the purchase of books. As the years went by several memorial funds were established for the specific purpose of improving the library, and there was increasing support from the general budget. In the decade from 1925 to 1935, the number of books and photographs doubled and the number of slides increased threefold. In 1953 the librarian could report that 29,000 books had been accessioned and some 93,000 slides circulated to the schools. The loans of slides and photographs to schools, churches, clubs, and other groups totalled 120,747 items in 1965. In that same year the library holdings in books and bound periodicals amounted to 55,275. The library receives over 600 leading periodicals from all over the world. Its lending collection has reached a total of some 197,000 items, of which over 100,000 are slides, and more than 93,000 are photographs, color reproductions, and postcards.

A department of photography was created in 1916. It produces postcards for the Museum's sales desk, slides, illustrations for the monthly *Bulletin* and other media of publicity, fills orders for requests that come from the outside, and photographs all acquisitions. The Museum also operates a print shop, and in 1958 the director established a conservation department, which gives expert attention to the fine art of maintaining, repairing, and restoring art objects of all kinds.[9]

The registrar's office checks and records all objects that come to the Museum or leave its collections for any reason and especially as loans to other institutions. The total number of purchases and gifts in the fifty years of the Museum's history is nearly 41,000. The registrar records all loans to and by the Museum and with the aid of the curators prepares catalogue cards for all objects in the Museum and maintains a running record of their condition and their coverage by insurance. At present the Museum carries insurance of $10,000,000 on the building, $5,000,000 on the works of art, and $500,000 to cover loans from institutions and collectors in the United States and Canada—amounts which fall far short of the actual value of the Museum's possessions. In 1964 the registrar handled 5,777 objects; 574 were permanent additions, 1,105 represented special exhibits, 1,370 had been sent to Cleveland for examination and study, presumably with a view to possible purchase, and 2,728 were entries for the May Show.

Besides its obligation to interpret its collections to the public, a museum also has an obligation to encourage and publish the scholarly research of its staff. In recent years, the Museum has encouraged scholarly publications in increasing numbers. As early as 1924 the Yale University Press published Langdon Warner's *Japanese Sculpture of the Suiko Period* for the Museum. Five trustees contributed the subsidy required to cover the cost of printing this first important book sponsored by the Museum. There followed a handbook and catalogue of the Severance armor collection, which received excellent reviews in leading papers in the East.[10] In 1944 the

Prentiss fund financed the book, *Islamic Art*. Ten years later Lee's *Chinese Landscape Painting*, a book-catalogue, appeared in both paperback and hardcover editions; a revised second edition was issued in 1962. Among recent Museum publications (several of which served as exhibition catalogues) are Lee's *Japanese Decorative Style* and *Ancient Sculpture from India*, Munro's *Evolution in the Arts*, Edward B. Henning's *Paths of Abstract Art*, Henry Hawley's *Neo-classicism: Style and Motif*, and Rémy Saisselin's *Style, Truth and the Portrait*. Books by staff members published outside the Museum have included Lee's *History of Far Eastern Art*, Munro's *Oriental Aesthetics*, and James Johnson's *The Radiance of Chartres*. In 1959 Merald Wrolstad joined the staff as editor and designer of the Museum's publications.

The sales desk performs an educational function for the many visitors, old and young, who come to the Museum to view its treasures. From a humble beginning as a small counter in the armor court the sales desk has grown into a business which grossed approximately $46,000 in 1965, and its receipts continue to grow. Here are sold art books of all kinds, the publications of the Museum, postcards, slides, prints, and reproductions of the Museum's prints and paintings. On its counters are displayed art books which appeal both to the student of art and to the interested layman and casual visitor; requests come from individuals, libraries, and museums from all over the world.

In the first forty years in the life of the Museum, 14,602,113 persons passed through its doors. In 1947 an eleven-year-old Amish girl from nearby Chardon came through the turnstile as the ten millionth visitor to the Museum and was presented with a Renoir reproduction in honor of the occasion. With the volume of traffic in and out of the Museum it is not difficult to appreciate the many responsibilities of the operations administrator, Albert J. Grossman, and of the staff members who maintain the building and grounds as a clean, secure, and safe place. It is unnecessary to detail the many aspects of the services that are part of the everyday tasks of operating and guarding the physical plant of the Museum. They include packing and shipping to and from the Museum—in 1964, the department of building and grounds handled 699 outgoing and 4,282 incoming items—and the maintenance of proper humidity in the galleries where too little would probably make the antique French furniture fall apart and too much would cause canvases to bulge and textiles to mildew. Hourly readings for humidity in the daytime and half-hourly at night were begun in 1922. "Washing" the air yielded a weekly accumulation of a bucket and a half of dirt.

The superintendent supervises the installment of special exhibits under the direction of Museum designer William Ward and the curators. The superintendent also is responsible for heating, lighting, and guarding of the galleries and storage rooms and the many other activities which are involved in the Museum's general housekeeping. In 1949 the Museum was air-conditioned at a time when only three other museums in this country were so equipped and more recently, 33 television cameras were installed to enable eight centrally-located monitors to keep all the galleries under constant surveillance. In 1956 the trustees appropriated $15,500 to fight termites. Over the years, much of the money for maintenance and physical improvements has come from the Huntington trust fund, whose chairman is Lewis B. Williams, a devoted friend of the Museum.

In a complex organization like the Cleveland Museum, labor relations are a matter of prime importance. In 1917 there were fourteen employees on the payroll; in 1966 there were 198. Smooth operation of the Museum depends not only on its professional staff but also on the porters, guards, maintenance and utility men who keep the plant in operation. The

National Labor Relations Act of the Roosevelt New Deal years which stimulated the growth of labor organizations and collective bargaining had its effect upon the personnel of the Museum. By 1937 the trustees found it necessary to create a special committee to work with the director and the superintendent on the whole problem of labor relations. Their findings revealed that the Cleveland Museum was open more hours a week than many other museums and that the wage scale needed adjustment. Organizers for the Building Services and Maintenance Union decided to try to enlist the labor force of the Museum in its Local Union #47, and demanded a forty-hour week, pay increases, an hour for lunch, extra pay for overtime, and an arbitration procedure to adjust disputes that might arise between employers and employees. Milliken was abroad at the time but admitted upon his return that the work week had been too long and that he was "trying to put our house in order." [11]

Harold Clark bore the brunt of the negotiations with the men. Even though the Wagner Act did not apply to the Museum, he readily recognized the right of the men to form a union and to bargain collectively. "We want a museum," he announced, "that is great not only in its fine building, its beautiful objects of art, but in its human relations both inside and outside the Museum." A new wage scale went into effect in November 1937. Further negotiations resulted in further wage increases in the 1940's, a special cost-of-living bonus in 1947, and other increases in pay that were tied to the fluctuations of the price index of the Bureau of Labor Statistics. A more generous pension system was established by the trustees in addition to participation in the social security system, and such fringe benefits as group and hospital insurance have been added. Agreement on a new wage scale in 1950 added $11,500 to the Museum's operating budget, and further increases have been made in the wages of porters, painters, engineers, and utility men. In 1965 the operating budget of the Museum showed that the expense for pensions was $72,-256; for social security, $34,523; for hospitalization, $40,789; and for group insurance, nearly $9,000.[12]

The number of Museum employees who have joined Local #47 is relatively small and represents a minority of those who would be eligible for membership. Nevertheless, the Museum authorities have never failed to grant a hearing for the union's complaints or demands. There is no written contract between the trustees and the union, only a number of verbal agreements which have never been violated. Since 1965 the Museum collects the dues of union members. Much of the credit for this relatively harmonious relationship between employers and employed must go to Clark for his intelligent and sympathetic approach to the whole problem of labor relations. He contributed anonymously on several occasions to social events sponsored by the union, and the union sent him a basket of fruit when he was ill in the hospital with pneumonia. Repeatedly the trustees have received letters from union officials in appreciation of the pleasant relations that continue to exist between the trustees and the labor organization, and almost invariably such letters singled out Clark for special thanks and commendation.

CHAPTER TEN

The Trials of a Director

T HE MOUTH OF every gift horse should be scientifically examined," wrote Charles L. Freer of Detroit on May 29, 1914, to the first director of the Cleveland Museum. He went on to caution against accepting anything from a donor just because he happens to be rich and advised asking him for money instead. In any case, however, "refuse in six pages." Freer's advice is as valid today as it was when the Museum began to assemble its collections.

Directors and curators are flooded with inquiries about objects whose value the writers are eager to ascertain. The Pennsylvania Museum of Art was the first in the United States to establish a special Bureau of Identification to deal with such inquiries and to furnish expert opinions.[1] "Do you buy relics?" asked an elderly lady in a letter to Whiting in 1920 and went on to offer to sell him a melodeon, a quilt, a knitting machine, and an "old, old spinning wheel." Missionaries home from the mission field brought back objects which they hoped to sell to the Museum, and there have been scores of inquiries to find out whether an art object is authentic or whether a battered violin found in a dusty attic might not be a genuine Stradivarius. The curators stand ready to give advice on everything except the monetary value of the object under consideration and they have been asked to make appraisals of objects ranging from the shoe buckles worn by the father of his country to a possible painting by Rembrandt.

A Philadelphia lawyer wrote Whiting on January 21, 1927, to offer for sale almost a thousand pieces, some of which were reputed to be 5,000 years old, and belonging to a client, "a scion of an old Italian family" who "recently migrated to America." In 1930 a resident of Florida offered to sell the Museum 1,223 pieces of South Slavic peasant art for $12,500.[2] A phony baroness brought a picture to Cleveland and claimed that J. H. Wade, who had died in the meantime, had wanted to buy it for his collection.[3] A restaurant owner in California inquired whether the Museum could reproduce an oil painting much admired by his customers so that it could be sold to department stores for a royalty, and an Irishman urged Director Lee to stop in the Emerald Isle to examine "crusts of a strange type of rock from the moons surface brought to earth by the fairies and Leprechauns . . . for curing desease [sic] of all type in cattle and horses."

As early as 1921, the director complained of the drainage upon the time and energy of his staff by requests to visit private homes to examine art objects. The trustees promptly ruled that they must be brought to the Museum for study and appraisal. From time to time the board has approved the disposal of objects that were of no value to the Museum. In 1929 James W. Packard's valuable collection of watches was transferred to the Horological Institute of America in Washington. On May 22, 1930, the Trustees voted "that it be the rule of the Museum not to accept any work of art as a gift from the artist." In 1945 the Museum, in conformity with the agreement with the Hurlbut trustees, sold a number of objects from the Hurlbut collection "stored here but not fit for exhibition."[4] In 1950 327 pieces of lace were disposed of, and in 1957 objects discarded from the Museum's collections included a saber from the Civil War, a model birch-bark canoe, a child's blocks, a straw hat, a halibut hook, three birds made of shells, and a number of unclaimed entries from past May Shows. Occasionally, the Museum staff also had to resist efforts to involve them in embarrassing discussions of the value of gifts claimed by the donors for tax exemption.

Problems arise unexpectedly in the delicate field of public relations. In 1921, for example, the Museum, for good reasons, shifted the time of its educational programs for adults from Wednesday to Friday evenings. Rabbi Wolsey of the Euclid Temple promptly protested that Friday had been preempted by his congregation for years for its regular Friday night lectures, and Whiting could only reply that the Museum stood ready to repeat the program on Wednesday evening, provided the rabbi's congregation would meet the additional expense.[5] In 1936 a social worker protested the Museum's sponsorship of a lecture on guns in connection with an exhibit of firearms.[6] On January 28, 1952, an indignant letter writer to *The Cleveland Press* challenged the Museum's purchase of Tintoretto's *Baptism of Christ* because it showed John the Baptist pouring water on Christ's head from a bowl, whereas "the fundamental God-given facts in the Bible" specify total immersion. A village pastor, visiting a museum for the first time in his life was so shocked by the nudes that he likened the Cleveland Museum to a House of Shame which was leading people, and especially children, to vice and ruin. He demanded a purge of all nudes from the Museum's galleries. This time the director was spared the chore of replying to the irate pastor for another letter to the editor informed the minister that "the body is God's temple" and "nothing is good or bad but thinking makes it so."[7] On a more pleasant occasion the Museum was the scene of a wedding of a young couple who had met in the garden court during an organ recital. Contrary to all Museum rules they managed to have the ceremony performed in these romantic surroundings.[8]

Rarely have donors been violently dissatisfied with the way the Museum used their money or displayed their gifts, but one such incident occurred in 1936 when a donor gave the Museum $25,000 for the purchase of a painting in memory of her husband. After careful study, the Museum decided to buy Paul Cézanne's *Pigeon Tower at Montbriand* as an addition to its then-weak collection of impressionist and post-impressionist paintings. This particular Cézanne had been exhibited at the Chicago World's Fair, among other places, where it was insured for $60,000. The donor's instructions had been to buy a "decent picture," an oil "by a well-known Master." She promptly notified the director of her and her dead husband's dislike for all of Cézanne's work although she admitted having given the Museum a free hand in making the selection. When she came to the Museum and found the label of the memorial to her husband still on the painting she tore it off in a burst of anger. Years after her death surviving relatives agreed to have the label restored.

The incident involving a sculpture by Max Kalish was of a quite different nature. Kalish (1891-1945), born in Poland and trained in the Cleveland School of Art, may be described as the sculptor of the working man. In much of his work he stressed the dignity of the worker and the impact of modern industry upon the laboring man. Among his creations was a little bronze, *The Angry Christ,* originally entitled *Jesus Views the Modern World.* It was a representation of the founder of Christianity far different from the traditional "gentle Jesus." In 1926 the bronze came to the Museum as an anonymous gift. Fifteen years later, the donor wrote the director to explain that in the meantime she had left the German Lutherans and become an Episcopalian, that she now considered it sinful "to make representations of Christ" and that she hoped the little statue could be melted down into the shape of a cross and given to a religious mission, thus removing the "blot on her conscience." Milliken refused to destroy the object but promised it would not be shown.

The majority of art dealers presumably are honest but many of them have become extraordinarily secretive because of the cut-throat competition in which they are forced to engage Frequently they encourage competition between museums and collectors as desirable art objects come on the market, and the rivalry among Italian dealers has on occasion been very intense. As a result of these practices it becomes more and more difficult to establish the actual value of an object, or to discover who originally owned it and the price he got for it. Nevertheless, dealers and art connoisseurs continue to perform a necessary function. "Does the public know enough to select its own fodder?" wrote one who made his living by "finding" art objects for museums and collectors. "Doesn't it rely on the carefully composed menu?" he continued.[9] The same writer, writing from Rome, deplored the disappearance of "the scholarly, experienced connoisseur art dealer."[10]

One reason for the difficulty in getting proper attributions for art objects was the regulation imposed by nationalist governments, and particularly Greece and Italy, which prohibited the export of art objects except with a license from the government. The result has been "bootlegging" of objects whose authorship must be kept nameless by the dealers. As early as 1925, the Museum's European representative advised that all references to price, country of origin, and prior ownership "as regards provenance" be omitted from the Museum's *Bulletin*. He charged that even such reliable dealers as Joseph Brummer and Jacob Hirsch were bootlegging things out of

Italy.[11] In 1934 the Museum was advised to get Japanese screens out of Japan as quietly as possible lest the government declare them national treasures and prohibit their exportation.

To aggravate the situation people began to gamble in art as they do in industrial stocks. Greek shipowners and Texas millionaires now compete with museums in world art markets, and the works of the masters are considered one of the best permanent forms of investment. The mania for buying for speculative purposes spawned a new crop of dealers, a rise in prices and excessive press-agenting—a kind of "racketeering in the art world," instead of an emphasis on beauty and culture.[12] Bidding at auctions became more intense and sometimes was done by undercover agents.

The problem of determining authenticity remained a difficult one despite improved methods of detecting forgeries by historical scholarship and physico-chemical tests. As early as 1931, James J. Rorimer published a book on the use of ultraviolet rays in the examination of works of art. Learned archaeologists and geologists have been mistaken and have written authentications for what turned out to be the work of modern forgers. By 1950 the customs regulations of the United States added to the problems of the art collector. An eighteenth-century clock, for example, was considered an object of utility and so could not be cleared as art by the customs office in Cleveland, but a painting produced in 1640 could be cleared although its frame had to be sent to Chicago. Modern sculpture was denied free entry if it did not represent "a natural object."[13]

The art world has heard many tales of skillful forgeries passed off on museums and collectors as genuine art treasures.[14] There was a rash of forgeries of ivories, "medieval" crosses, crucifixes, and paintings after World War II, and the indiscriminate buying of art objects by wealthy industrialists

Directors

Frederic Allen Whiting
1913–1930

Sherman Emery Lee
1958–

William Mathewson Milliken
1930–1958

View from Euclid Avenue, across the lagoon.

Aerial view of
the Museum and
the Fine Arts Garden.

The Special Exhibition Galleries.

The Armor Court.

contributed to the scandals. The director of a Rarity Research Society in Detroit apparently made a business of separating "the lies from the truth," for a price.[15] More scientific was the European Faelscher-Verband, a society of museum directors organized to expose forgeries. Milliken was an active member, and when the organization was revived after World War II accepted the presidency of the rejuvenated society.[16]

The Cleveland Museum suffered less than many museums from dealers who either knowingly or unwittingly peddled forgeries as genuine articles, but one experience, the Dossena affair, attracted national and international attention. Alceo Dossena came from a poor family in Cremona, Italy, and began his remarkable career as a stonecutter's apprentice. A veteran of World War I, he eventually settled in Rome and it was here that he did his notable work as a sculptor and woodcarver and here he died in 1937. Parsons described him as "a real artist," "a genius," "the greatest forger who ever lived," who worked like the great masters of old and yet was "a simple man who was born and died poor, exploited . . . by unscrupulous dealers." [17]

In May 1927 the Cleveland Museum bought what was certified to be "a genuine Archaic Greek statue of Athena, dating from about 480 B.C.," from the dealer Jacob Hirsch for $120,000.[18] Hirsch asserted he had bought the statue in Geneva in 1926 and in the provenance furnished the Museum he stated that he knew the owner of the land on which the marble statue had been excavated secretly in the dead of night. He suggested that it would be best to say the marble pieces had come from the Aegean Islands rather than from Tarentum in Italy. This would maintain the secrecy of the excavations which seemed especially important because the dealer had been promised first claim on any new discoveries.

The Museum acquired the *Athena* on the unqualified recommendation of Parsons, who continued to defend its genuineness even after doubts had been raised about its authenticity.[19] In December 1927 he wrote, "The matter of the *Athena* must not be hurried . . . there is no evidence of its fake origin." His letter noted that leading German archaeologists had pronounced that statue genuine. It was not until April 1928 that Parsons advised returning the *Athena* to the dealer, who agreed to refund the purchase price.[20]

The second piece involved in this international scandal was a large wooden statue of a *Madonna and Child,* supposedly by Giovanni Pisano. Its purchase also had been recommended by the Museum's European representative.[21] It was bought with $18,500 from the Huntington fund. Its authenticity was challenged first in a letter from W. R. Valentiner of the Detroit Institute of Arts to Milliken on March 30, 1926. The director of the Cleveland Museum had described the statue as "superb," "by the hand of a master and if not by Giovanni himself by one worthy to be called his equal."[22] Nevertheless, an X-ray examination showed the statue was held together with nails and stuffed with old papers. It was returned to the dealer and the money refunded.

Details of the unsavory business came to light when Dossena announced he had been cheated by dealers who commissioned him to copy originals which they sold abroad without proper compensation for their creator. Several other American museums, including the Boston Museum and the Frick Collection of New York, also were victims of these shady transactions, and Whiting took comfort from the thought that the fraud was discovered by the Cleveland Museum "before the storm burst" in the press.[23]

The Dossena forgeries were a sensation from coast to coast and abroad. *The Rocky Mountain News* carried a headline "Millions Paid for Fake Art Made in Italy."[24] *The New York Times* called for sounder scholarship in the art world and estimated the total of fraudulent sales at $2,175,000. The

London *Art Weekly* exposed the forgeries of the masterpieces of Tuscan Renaissance art in a long article.[25] Dossena had produced the effect of erosion so successfully that leading archaeologists and geologists were misled completely.

The only other comparable incident in the history of the Museum that became an international sensation concerned the purchase in 1959 of Rubens' *Diana and Her Nymphs Departing for the Chase,* a painting bought with money from the Leonard C. Hanna Jr. Bequest. When J. Paul Getty, often referred to as the world's richest man, bought another *Diana* in 1961 for $400,000, a question arose immediately as to who had the original and who a copy. The discussion among art connoisseurs was blown up by the press into an international sensation. Both paintings were authenticated by leading European experts. On the other hand, Jean Neger, a Paris dealer, attacked Ludwig Burchard, the leading authority who had authenticated the Cleveland Rubens, and broadcast copies of his sensational pamphlet to museums, directors, trustees, F.B.I., and police chiefs throughout the United States.

Director Lee insisted that the Cleveland Museum had a genuine Rubens, and Francis, the curator of paintings, who had traced the history of the painting back to 1796, declared every brushstroke was by the master himself. Champions of the Getty painting traced this version back to 1655 to a Spanish ambassador in Belgium who was a friend of the painter. Getty brought Professor Julius S. Held, a Rubens expert from Barnard College, to England to authenticate his picture and Held concluded that the Cleveland painting was made by an assistant but that Rubens may have participated in the work. It is common knowledge that the master had a workshop in Antwerp where he employed a number of painters who helped him fill orders that came faster than he could fill them. The American professor contended that there was more from Rubens' own hand in the Getty than in the Cleveland paint-

117

ing. On the other hand, Michael Jaffe, art historian of Cambridge University in England, came to the opposite conclusion and maintained that the Cleveland Museum not only had the original *Diana,* but that it was the work of Rubens himself. In this he agreed with the late Ludwig Buchard, admittedly the leading authority on Rubens.

On September 28, 1959, *Life* magazine had reported the Cleveland purchase from a New York dealer. British papers asked how such a "national treasure" had gotten out of the country without a permit from the Board of Trade.[26] On February 12, 1962, *Life* stirred the embers of controversy again in a profusely illustrated article entitled "The Dilemma of Diana's Double." Thereupon the matter received nationwide publicity, some of it serious, much of it facetious.[27]

The director of the Cleveland Museum had maintained from the outset that both paintings probably were authentic. In April 1962 Lee visited Getty in England. His examination of the painting confirmed his original judgment. The battle of the two *Dianas* has faded into history and each owner seems to be satisfied with his own. During the argument gratuitous advice came from many connoisseurs, professional and amateur. One deserves recording. A Californian urged the use of her swinging pendulum test (apparently something like a divining rod), which proved decisively that Cleveland had the genuine and original Rubens and suggested that henceforth the director would be well advised to use this method of establishing the authenticity of all future acquisitions.[28]

Only rarely has the Museum found itself in possession of art objects which were acquired in good faith and turned out to have been stolen. One such incident involved a carved ivory book cover bought in 1928 for $30,000 from a New York dealer and found later to have been stolen by a bogus "count" from the Cathedral of Agram in Zagreb. The thief had persuaded the bell-ringer to let him live and work in the cathedral for a year, ample time to steal and to replace jewels in precious art objects with worthless glass. The Museum returned the ivory with great ceremony to the Yugoslav minister who came to Cleveland for the occasion. The restitution was effected in a ceremony in the trustees' room of the Museum decorated for the occasion with the American and Yugoslav flags. The dealer reimbursed the Museum.[29]

In 1950 the Museum returned a section of an abbot's cape stolen from the Diocesan Museum in Barcelona in 1936 during the Spanish Revolution. The research of Dorothy Shepherd, curator of textiles, traced the object to its original owner and the director of the Museum was decorated by the Spanish government in gratitude for its return.[30] Ten years later, the United States Treasury Department broke up a ring that had been smuggling Chinese art objects into the country from abroad. The Museum had refused to buy two scrolls which had been offered for sale.[31]

In the many volumes of the trustees' minutes only one reference has been found to a theft of an art object from the Museum itself, in this case a ring valued at $12.50, stolen from the American Indian room in 1939.[32] In 1955 however, a mysterious theft occurred which made good copy for newspapers far and wide. In June of that year the Junior Council staged a Mid-European street fair with tents, dancers, a midway, and other features to raise money for the Museum. The event was widely advertised in the press, including the city's foreign-language publications. One of the fair's special attractions was an exhibit of the famous Salvador Dali jewels including *The Royal Heart* of gold which opened upon a smaller pulsating heart run by an electric motor and surrounded by precious stones. To see this and other fantastic creations visitors were charged fifty cents, half to go to the Museum and half to the Catherwood Foundation of Bryn Mawr which owned the collection.

Suddenly the press got a story that *The Eye of Time,* a $6,000 creation of the eccentric Spanish surrealist, had disappeared from the collection. The presumption was that it had been stolen, although the object was kept in a special case provided by the Foundation. Dali accused the Museum guards of negligence. The inspector of police described the incident as "a publicity stunt." Before long the director of the Museum received a postcard promising the return of the jewel if the matter could be dropped, and just as the exhibit was about to close the jewel was returned by mail in a cigar box with paper wrappings and twelve cents postage due. The mystery was never solved. *The Erie Sunday Times* of July 24, 1955, commented wryly that the jewels were beautiful and delightful to see but that Dali's "real field . . . seems to be a knack for publicity." [33]

The case of the Dijon *Mourners* points to another problem which the directors of the Cleveland Museum fortunately have had to face but once. In the Ducal Palace of Dijon, France, are the tombs of two of the Dukes of Burgundy, Philip the Bold, and John the Fearless. Their tombs are decorated by a procession of mourners, little statues carved in the fifteenth century. In 1795 fanatics of the French Revolution ordered the beheading of all stone images of dead despots but the tombs in Dijon were somehow saved from destruction. Some twenty-five years later when they were rehabilitated, thirteen of the mourners were found to be missing. Four, it was discovered later, had been sold to a collector in New York, at whose death two came into the possession of Leonard C. Hanna Jr., and thence to the Cleveland Museum, and two were acquired directly by the Museum.

Although there could be no question about the title, *The Toledo Blade* began a crusade to have the four mourners returned to Dijon in the interest of more cordial Franco-American relations. Milliken quite properly refused to return the quartet missing from the tombs and contended that it would be impossible to make casts of them without spoiling the finish of the originals. Eventually, however, Italian craftsmen made exact duplicates, and Director Lee personally delivered the casts in Dijon with an appropriate speech in French. The incident came to a happy close when the French museum replaced the old label, "Au Musée de Cleveland," with a new one that indicated that the figures were the gift of The Cleveland Museum of Art.[34]

There remains the problem of contemporary art and the task of the director to steer a middle course between those who want to stay with the traditional forms of representational art and those who would fill the Museum with the latest abstract creations. The Museum is under no obligation to endorse all it shows in its galleries, but it has a responsibility to acquaint the public with new developments in the field of art as noted by competent critics and shown in other places so that the public eventually may decide what it regards as ephemeral and what is likely to endure. By their charters some museums have not been permitted to acquire art objects until twenty or twenty-five years after the artist's death. Fortunately no such restrictions bind the Cleveland Museum and it has purchased contemporary art from the beginning and especially from its own May Show.

In 1908 there was an exhibit in New York of the work of a school of painters who believed that nothing was too undignified to be unworthy of their talents. They were promptly labeled "the Ashcan School." Alfred Kazin referred to them and their confreres in literature as "specialists in anguish." The often brutal frankness of the paintings of these artists foreshadowed the era of materialism and cynical disillusion which followed World War I.

In the year in which the Cleveland Museum was incorporated the Armory Show "exploded" in New York and touched off a storm in which conservatives raged against the "extremism" of many of the exhibits. Here were modernists of all varieties—impressionists, post-impressionists, futurists, cubists, and others. Here Cézanne, Matisse, and Picasso were damned by the traditionalists. None other than Theodore Roosevelt visited the show on the day Woodrow Wilson was inaugurated as President, and wrote his impressions for *The Outlook*. With the skill and caution of the practiced politician he pleaded for fair play for the progressives and condemned the work of "the lunatic fringe." Whatever the ultimate verdict, the Armory Show helped make art a subject of popular interest and discussion. Art became fashionable in America as in France, and the public gradually became more acclimated to new experiments with color and form. It is well to remember that all art once was contemporary, and it is interesting to recall that the Paris police had to put down a riot precipitated by the impressionist exhibition of 1876. The Armory Show introduced some painters who now are regarded as old masters.[35]

Milliken was not impressed with what he saw at the International Exhibition of Paintings in Vienna in the 1920's. He referred to Italian "horrors" made "with pieces of fabric mixed with paint" and he was equally repelled by "the flagrant vulgarity and extreme radicalism" of the Germans and Russians.[36] As early as 1921, the Cleveland Museum had an exhibition of French impressionist art and an exhibit of contemporary American painting. Milton S. Fox, a member of the Museum's staff and the art critic for *The Cleveland News*, deplored the fact that the Museum seemed to have only a very moderate interest in the "radicalism" of modern art,[37] but six years later the galleries were opened to an exhibition of cubism, surrealism, Dadaism, and abstract art generally, which was circulated by New York's Museum of Modern Art. One painting had the arresting title of *A Chemist*

Lifting with Precaution the Cuticle of a Grand Piano.[38] By 1939 Milliken had overcome his aversion to "extremism" and defended abstract art in a lecture in Pittsburgh. He was reported to have said, "There is nothing which says that a work of art is only something which we can recognize."[39]

In the 1940's some trustees as well as members of the Advisory Council exerted pressure upon the Museum staff to give more attention to modern art. One member of the council prepared a report on modern painting and listed painters whose work she believed the Museum should buy. In 1944 a group of women started the Venture Club to raise funds which the director could use to "gamble" on the work of little-known painters and thus promote "a progressive viewpoint toward the unfamiliar."[40]

In 1958 the Museum exhibited paintings and sculpture which emphasized the abstract expressionism of the post-World-War-II years. *The Plain Dealer* warned the public it would be "amazed," "puzzled" and "shocked."[41] The catalogue for the exhibition included an essay on abstract painting by Munro, which *The Akron Beacon Journal* of November 30, 1958, found rather unconvincing, and although the paper praised the director of the Museum for arranging the exhibit, the writer of the article concluded that "he does a rather thorough job of apologizing for his own temerity in authorizing such a display." The verbal cannonading about "art by anthropoid apes" continued in Cleveland for several weeks, although exhibits of this kind no longer were considered radical in some other cities.

In 1960 the trustees appropriated $15,000 to be spent specifically on avant-garde art, a sum that was increased substantially in later years.[42] The Museum continued to exhibit abstract paintings and ultra-modern sculpture and in 1960 arranged an exhibition to illustrate the various stages in the transition from representational art to abstractions. The educational process was a slow and difficult one, however. When the Ben Heller exhibition of abstract expressionist art came to Cleveland in 1962, disgusted viewers demanded that such "dirty and foul canvasses" be removed from the walls of the Museum.[48] Instead, the trustees approved a new curatorship for contemporary art, and Edward B. Henning, assistant to the director, was appointed to the new position in 1962. One of his first efforts was an essay on various attitudes toward modern art for the October 1963 *Bulletin*.

Letter writers occasionally still write the director to urge him to get rid of his "modern purchasing department" and stop buying "garbage,"[44] and a former Communist contended that the aim of the party is to remove all inspiring and beautiful art objects from American museums and substitute the "degenerate art" and "meaningless emptiness" of the abstractionists. Some still hold that the Cleveland Museum lags behind other institutions in the attention it gives to contemporary art.

The historian, who is neither an art critic nor a psychiatrist competent to uncover the hidden springs of an artist's creations, can only await the judgment of time. He is aware of what the curator of paintings aptly called "the human norm of suspicion toward things unfamiliar." He also knows that over the long years many fighting faiths have lost their champions and been forgotten. On the other hand, the radicalism of one generation often has become the conservatism of the next, and this may be as true of art as it has been in politics and economics. Meantime, the staff of a museum must somehow reconcile its own preferences with the obligation to introduce the public to the innovations of a changing age.

CHAPTER ELEVEN

Two Wars and a Depression

W ORLD WAR I was the first major war to involve the emotions and sympathies of America's nationality groups in the fortunes of their former fatherlands. Anglo- and Franco-Americans ardently hoped for a victory of the Allied Powers at war with Germany and did all they could to help bring it about. German- and many Irish-Americans were equally vocal in expressing their sympathy for the Central Powers. For three years, until the United States entered the war in April 1917 as a belligerent on the side of the Allies, Americans engaged in an acrimonious debate over the neutrality of the Wilson Administration. The cold draft of war blew across the American melting pot and not only retarded the fusion process which had been going on for years but brought about a recrystallization along internal lines of fracture which were not closed again until the United States in 1917 called on all citizens, regardless of national origins, to support the war with Germany.

America's entry into the war brought a violent, hysterical, and concerted demand to eradicate everything of German origin from American civilization. The movement was led by a minority of extremists but a large part of the population approved of "the drive against Teutonism." Mob rule broke out in many places. German music, art, books, church services, singing societies, and social clubs, the German language, indeed everything that could be labeled with the hated German name or traced to a German origin, came under the ban, as the passions of war threatened to divide the nation into pro- and anti-German groups. Hyphen-hunting became a popular pastime of overheated patriots, and the hysteria reached such absurd limits as to discard the time-honored wedding marches of Wagner and Mendelssohn, eliminate Bismarck herring from restaurant menus, trace the origin of the pretzel to Italy, rename sauerkraut "liberty cabbage," and substitute "liberty steak" for hamburger.

Cleveland was not immune from these hysterical reactions of misguided patriots. Its German language daily, *Wächter und Anzeiger,* was a major target of attack. Once a successful advertising medium for German readers, the paper now contained only a few want ads as the result of an advertisers' boycott. Circulation continued to shrink. Boy Scouts burned the "Hun" paper, riotous crowds interfered with its distribution by news agencies, the editors received threatening letters, two former editors were interned, and bundles of papers shipped to other towns mysteriously disappeared from trains and interurbans. Cleveland's English-language dailies kept up an unrelenting attack on their German competitor, and schoolteachers advised their pupils not to carry the paper. The American Protective League and the women of the American Relief Legion joined in organizing a boycott of all businesses and agencies that continued to deal with the German daily. In nearby Baldwin-Wallace College, students demonstrated against the singing of *Silent Night* at a Christmas celebration, eventually forcing the president's removal.[1]

In contrast with these turbulent events, affairs at the Cleveland Museum were relatively quiet during the war. It is remarkable and commendable that the anti-German hysteria so rampant on the outside did not penetrate the Museum walls. There is no evidence in the files that the institution's holdings in the field of German art came under fire from an excited public and no demand that they be removed from the galleries.

Ten months to the day after the Cleveland Museum was opened Congress declared war on the Central Powers. The war had its effect on the young institution, but with few exceptions it was able to continue its program largely unhampered by what was going on overseas. Some members resigned or were in arrears because of the war and the trustees voted, under certain circumstances, to remit dues for the duration. The *Bulletin* called for continued support for the Museum so that it might satisfy the need for "the comfort and the diversion of beauty and of the finer things of life, if the country . . . is to retain its sanity." [2]

Long before the building was ready for occupancy Director Whiting wrote Brand Whitlock, American Minister to Belgium, and offered to store Belgium's art treasures in his new fireproof building. Whitlock appreciated the offer but found it impractical to accept.[3] A similar suggestion to accept British art objects for safekeeping, provided Great Britain paid for insurance and transportation both ways, also was declined.[4]

During the war the flags of the Allied Nations were displayed in the rotunda of the Museum, war posters advertised the Liberty Loans, and employees could arrange for the purchase of war bonds through payroll deductions. Groups of adults and children met in the Museum to sing patriotic songs, and for the patriotic program in 1918 held on the steps of the building to commemorate Bastille Day Myron T. Herrick was one of the speakers. In October 1918 the galleries had to be closed for two weeks on orders from the health commissioner because of the influenza epidemic. In the fall of 1918 the Museum organized an exhibit of British and French war posters and lithographs which were displayed in four galleries along with the work of a number of war prisoners. The purpose was to whip up enthusiasm for the Fourth Liberty Loan, and the "final battle between materialism and idealism." [5] It is interesting to note that Harold Clark, who was with the peace commission in Paris on the staff of Bernard Baruch, wrote several letters from abroad to stress the need to plan for the preservation of records and relics of the war and for an appropriate war memorial in Cleveland.

Eleven years after the close of World War I the collapse of the stock market touched off the Great Depression of the 1930's, the longest and most severe economic collapse in our history. Like President Hoover, the director of the Cleveland Museum and a goodly number of his trustees predicted an early return to the prosperity of the booming 1920's; and from another point of view, Max Kalish, the Cleveland sculptor of the workingman, proclaimed his faith in the American worker, who "can be depended on to pull us through." [6] The optimists turned out to be false prophets indeed as the country sank ever deeper into the economic morass of the 1930's.

The Museum was more seriously affected by the Great Depression than it had been by the war. Bequests from the Severance, Mather, Prentiss, and other estates shrank with the collapse of the stock market and some of the banks, and the settlement of several estates had to be held in abeyance by trustees and trust officers until a recovery could restore them to something like their normal worth. The return on the Museum's investments was down sharply and purchases had to be curtailed. The yield of the Wade fund, for example, dropped from $141,373 in 1930 to $13,604 in 1934 and did not reach $150,000 again until 1950. Moreover the Wade fund included 660 shares of stock in a defunct Cleveland bank and this involved double liability of the stockholder. Payment by the Museum of the stock assessment was finally made in four annual installments.[7]

The trustees found it necessary to consent to an extension of time for the payment of principal and interest upon pledges to the general endowment fund held by another bank that also was in trouble and to agree to refunding where companies could not redeem their bonds when they came due. In case a will called for the sale of property for the benefit of the Museum the trustees were likely to await the return of better times.[8] The membership rolls continued to decline, and sales from the May Show dropped to $4,729 in 1932.[9] When vacancies occurred in the normal course of events in the staff of the Museum the positions were left unfilled and in 1933 all salaries above $1,200 were cut on a sliding scale from 2.5% to 15% in an effort to balance the budget.[10]

The average financial returns from an artist's life are not great even when times are good, and it requires little imagination to understand the artist's plight in a time of acute and prolonged depression. To provide some temporary relief an artists' curb market was held in the summer of 1932 on a vacant lot not far from the Museum. The event had many of the features of a street fair, with artists' models, music and refreshments. About 400 artists exhibited their wares to some 12,000 people; some objects were sold at public auction, others privately, and sales reached a total of $4,000. Sketches by Henry G. Keller sold for $1.00 and $1.50, and oil paintings for as low as $1.25. Few sales yielded as much as $75, and "quick sketch artists" did landscapes, silhouettes, and other drawings for almost any price.[11] A second market was held in 1933 in a tent behind Severance Hall where in a carnival atmosphere art objects again were offered at bargain prices.[12] The third annual curb market occurred indoors and reached

129

its climax in a costume ball, for which the admission charge was fifty cents.[13]

By this time the Roosevelt New Deal had its own program for the relief of unemployed and impecunious artists. It was the first frank recognition by government that artists had something to give to society and that society had a responsibility to art. In 1933 a public works of art project directed by the Treasury Department and financed with funds from the Civil Works Administration was established. Four thousand artists were employed. By the following summer they had produced 700 murals and over 15,000 other art works for schools, hospitals, courthouses and other public buildings. Most of their creations were based on native themes drawn from American history. Next the Treasury sponsored a painting and sculpture section for the decoration of federal buildings and employed such artists as Thomas Hart Benton and Rockwell Kent to supervise the work. Again the artists' murals illustrated both the pleasant and the seamy side of American life. Some painters however seemed so unmindful of the stark realities of the Depression as to continue to paint factory furnaces billowing black smoke and mills swarming with eager workmen.

In 1935 the Works Progress Administration established the Federal Art Project. In its four years it provided relief for over 5,000 artists. The beneficiaries of this fund not only painted more murals but gave free art classes to some 60,000 children a month and supervised community art centers visited by 6,000,000 people. The work of the artists was of varying merit, of course, but their efforts helped to foster an appreciation and understanding of art and to close the gap between the old masters and the moderns. Even commercial houses began to employ painters of murals, and in this age of experimentation with American art, in the words of Professor Arthur M. Schlesinger, "time dulled the edge of unfamiliarity." Many painters painted in a mood of depression, but Milliken, in a speech in Pittsburgh, described much of the art work created by artists on relief as "a healthy reaction from Parisian influence." [14]

In Cleveland Milliken was appointed regional director of the PWA artists' relief program in 1933. It was his responsibility to recruit painters, sculptors, and craftsmen to decorate the public buildings in this area. A long line of applicants appeared at the Director's office. Forty were selected and asked to submit sketches. The Cleveland quota finally was fixed at 69, and more than twice that number applied for employment. There was keen competition for the coveted assignments and some applicants were fearful that the committee to select the winners would favor the "moderns." The Cleveland committee who did the selecting included John L. Severance, Mrs. Malcolm McBride, Mrs. B. P. Bole, and others prominent in Cleveland art and Museum circles. Artists fortunate enough to be chosen to work for the government were paid from $25 to $40 a week. They produced eight murals for the Cleveland Public Library, plaques for schools, historical maps, and other art objects. In March 1934 the Museum had an exhibit of some 150 items produced by 72 artists. William Sommer painted a mural for the Public Library which represented the city and its Public Square as it was a hundred years ago; other murals depicted Cleveland's waterfront along Lake Erie in 1835 and the bridges spanning the Cuyahoga River. [15]

In 1935 the Government allotted specific sums for murals in post-office buildings. Although the awards were made on a competitive basis and were based on unsigned sketches by the competing artists there were unwarranted complaints of favoritism by a federal bureaucracy. [16] In 1936 WPA put 75 Cleveland artists to work in an old factory building, making signs, lantern slides, paintings, and sculpture. [17] Whatever some of his trustees may have thought of the "boondoggling" and waste of tax money by the New Deal, Milliken enthusiastically supported the government's several attempts to spread its protective wings over artists in their time of hardship and deprivation. In 1938 the debate over a plan to create a permanent federal arts division supported by a government subsidy produced the absurd charge that the proposal was a clever device of radical artists to spread communism in the United States.

Despite the herculean efforts of the Roosevelt Administration to lift the country out of the economic doldrums by hitherto-untried remedies the United States really did not emerge from the prolonged Depression until it became involved in the Second World War, first as a supplier of war material to friendly nations and then as an active belligerent in the war itself. Hitler plunged Europe into war in 1939; Pearl Harbor occurred two years later and the American people found themselves committed to total war in the Pacific as well as on the continent of Europe.

War-born prosperity finally pulled the nation out of the Great Depression, although war brought new problems of even greater magnitude. With the exception of the treatment of Japanese Nisei on the West Coast the Second World War brought no repetition of the public hysteria of the First, although World War II constituted a much greater drain on national resources than 1917 and 1918 had done, and the American people lived in constant fear that cities and industrial centers like Cleveland might be the targets for bombing raids by enemy fliers.

The Museum had been careful not to become involved in the war of propaganda which preceded the fighting and was continued throughout the war by German Nazis and Italian fascists and their misguided sympathizers in the United States. During the Ethiopian crisis when Italy invaded Haile Selassie's kingdom, Milliken had been critical of what he considered England's pose as the savior of the world through the League of Nations, but his great love for Italy did not keep him from pointing out that there was both right and wrong on Italy's side. Like many Americans who credited Mussolini with driving the beggars off the streets and getting the trains on time the director of the Cleveland Museum found his beloved Italy a haven of serenity, comfort, and friendliness before the war in contrast with a world in turmoil and torn by strife between capital and labor.[18] In 1938 Munro, in an address to the National Education Association, argued that art should be used to make peace glamorous instead of war.[19] As late as the fall of 1939, the Museum's trustees refused a request from the Institute of Modern Art of Boston for an exhibit of German art objects outlawed by the Nazis on the ground that it was not the business of the Museum to become involved in propaganda of any kind.[20]

Such discussions were largely academic even before Pearl Harbor. The Board of Trustees resolved to keep the Museum open at all costs during the war, to avoid panic, and to build morale, but urged the staff to prepare for any eventuality and to make plans to list, pack, store, and remove art objects in case of an enemy attack.[21] In September 1942 the first page of the Museum's *Bulletin* was devoted to "The Museum's Mobilization for Victory." The article described exhibits dealing with the war and the United Nations including pictures of the Fire Blitz of London and drawings by children in the occupied areas of Europe which had been collected by the American Friends Service Committee. A member of the Museum's staff worked with the civilian camouflage committee; others were active in preparing war posters and other visual aids to mobilize popular support for the war, or helped train air-raid wardens in Cleveland's manufacturing plants. The *Bulletin* also stressed the function of the Museum as a recreational and social service center, "to prevent the increase of juvenile delinquency in a warring nation."

Attendance at the Museum dropped notably during the war, partly because of gas rationing and the need to conserve automobile tires. The May Show was smaller than usual and to reduce expenses the Museum charged every entrant a fee of one dollar. As teachers were drawn into various patriotic activities the schools made less use of the Museum's services, particularly slides and exhibits. Members of the Museum staff were on leave with the Armed Forces and others went into defense work.

In January 1942 the Office of Civilian Defense inquired into what artists could contribute to the war effort in the area of camouflage, patriotic posters, and retraining for defense work. The next month Milton S. Fox of the education department of the Museum published a pamphlet on the artist's role in a total war. The trustees authorized the director to work out a plan to protect the Museum's treasures from air raids and appropriated $2,000 for "defense preparations," to buy sand, pumps, hose, fire extinguishers, and shutters for windows. Some works of art were removed to a "treasure room" in the basement which was protected by three floors of concrete. Boxes were built to contain art objects and the staff was drilled to take up their posts and perform their appointed tasks in case of an attack. Pails of water and other fire-fighting equipment were placed in strategic positions. A first-aid room was set up, and there were periodic blackouts and drills for the fire and rescue squads. Because a number of porters were in service the director equipped each office with brooms and dust cloths so that the personnel could perform the necessary janitorial work. A victory vegetable garden replaced the garden of flowers around the Museum and about 28,000 square feet were brought under cultivation.

An exhibit entitled Can America Be Bombed? was arranged

for July 1942 to illustrate the basic facts of air warfare and to prepare Clevelanders for total war. Sixty-eight pieces of "refugee art" that had been left stranded in San Francisco's Golden Gate Exposition when war broke out in Europe, were stored for safekeeping, at great expense, in the Cleveland Museum.[22] While all these war activities were going on in an atmosphere of great excitement, Munro, in a lead article in the *Bulletin* of February 1942, re-emphasized the primary duty of the Museum to build public morale, and to be "a symbol of enlightened, unselfish democracy," through exhibits which reveal a "broad-minded liberalism, the international attitude of our people [and] our respect for all forms of religious and artistic expression." When the Nazis forbade the exhibit of work by Jewish artists in Holland, Milliken hung Joseph Israel's *Woman Making Cakes* in the armor court of the Museum, where it could be displayed most prominently.[23] In 1943 the Museum opened its auditorium to the Air Corps cadets of Western Reserve University for instructional purposes.

Fortunately, Cleveland never had to put its preparations for defense against aerial warfare to the test of an enemy attack. Unfortunately, however, victory in World War II was followed by an uneasy peace marked by acute tension between the United States and Russia and a "cold war" which threatened on several occasions to plunge the world into another shooting war, this time with weapons that could lead to the destruction of civilization itself. The peril is not yet ended, and it was acutely felt in the decade following the close of World War II. In 1950 the trustees of the Cleveland Museum considered a confidential report of the Metropolitan Museum of New York and the National Gallery in Washington on what to do in case of another war. Among other things the report described a plan to use mines and caves to protect works of art from destruction. In Cleveland, architect J. Byers Hays

135

was instructed not only to prepare plans for an addition to the Museum but also for its protection in the event of World War III.[24] He made various suggestions and recommended building an underground storage vault as part of the proposed addition to the Museum.

What is surprising in all this excitement before, during, and after the Second World War is the almost total absence of demands from the public that the Museum ban the exhibition of German and Russian art. The minutes of the Board of Trustees refer to only one incident, and that before the war, in 1936, when the director received a letter from a member of the American Federation of Teachers protesting the display of an exhibition of Five Centuries of German Art sponsored by the Carl Schurz Memorial Foundation of Philadelphia. The writer considered the exhibit Nazi propaganda and criticized the Museum for devoting too much of its programs to "real or fancied German cultural activities." Milliken replied that he was a strong anti-Nazi, that the exhibit was not propaganda, and that the Museum is interested in the art of all nations and not in matters of race, politics, or religion.[25] Fifteen years later, the director discussed the likelihood of another war with Vladimir Simkhovitch, professor of economic history at Columbia University, art collector and friend of the Cleveland Museum, and a donor to its library, building, and endowment funds. Milliken considered such a tragedy unlikely, deplored "too much hysteria" but concluded he would be sharply criticized if he failed to take precautions for another emergency.[26]

136

CHAPTER TWELVE

New Horizons

FOR SOME YEARS before World War II, it was apparent that the Cleveland Museum was rapidly outgrowing its physical resources. Art objects which the staff would have liked to exhibit had to be kept in storage. The library badly needed additional stack space. New rooms for the proper display of a growing collection of historic furniture were required. Administrative offices, storage vaults, and service quarters were no longer adequate for the growing business of the Museum. The lecture program and the activities of the department of education could be expanded to the profit of the entire community, provided additional space and personnel could be found. It is remarkable that without an active public campaign to solicit contributions for this specific purpose, a building fund for a new wing which would double the area of the original building came into existence almost spontaneously as the voluntary effort of donors, large and small, who appreciated the value of the Museum as an educational institution in the cultural life of this part of the country.

The first substantial contribution to a specific building

fund was made in 1937 by Mrs. Edward B. Greene, daughter of J. H. Wade II. Her initial gift of $20,000 was followed by annual contributions. In 1944 President Mather appointed a building committee, with Leonard C. Hanna Jr. as chairman. In four years the building fund grew to $450,000, and by 1950 it was approaching $1,500,000.[1] In 1954 a letter from the director describing crowded conditions in the Museum produced $420,000 in three weeks.[2] The minutes of the Board of Trustees show an increasing concern with the necessity of adding to the original structure. On several occasions the trustees voted to transfer substantial amounts from bequests like the Rogers and Prentiss funds to the building fund. Gifts from the Hanna Fund, of which Leonard C. Hanna Jr. was the president, eventually totaled nearly $6,400,000 of which $4,-000,000 went to the building fund to "match" voluntary contributions from other sources. More than $1,500,000 from the Huntington fund was used to help "match" the Hanna donations.

In 1953 the trustees of the Huntington Art and Polytechnic Trust petitioned the Cuyahoga County Common Pleas Court for permission to close the Huntington Polytechnic Institute and create in its stead a Huntington Fund for Education to aid deserving students who otherwise could not go to college to acquire scientific and technical training. At the time of the filing of the petition Clark was president of both the Museum and the Institute.

The original Huntington bequest envisioned both an art museum and a polytechnical school but the petition pointed out that it would be impossible to use enough Huntington money to provide an adequate building and faculty for the Polytechnic Institute without seriously hurting the Museum which needed the money for a new wing. The assets of the Huntington trust, it was argued, were not enough to properly support both institutions. Moreover the petition pointed out

138

that Cleveland now had a number of educational facilities to provide technical training for deserving students which did not exist when the Institute opened its doors in 1918. Since its founding, it had served some 60,000 students, but its major function under present conditions, it was argued, could be achieved best by awarding scholarships to qualified students in need of financial assistance that would enable them to attend the schools of their choice.

On August 11, 1953, to the dismay of some of the Institute's devoted alumni, Judge Donald F. Lybarger ruled that "a fund for charitable educational purposes to be known as the John Huntington Fund for Education" could be established "in lieu of operating an industrial training school." The decision made it possible to apply substantial amounts of Huntington money to the building fund of the Museum, and at the same time, it enabled the Huntington Fund for Education to grant significant amounts of scholarship aid to students in a number of schools.[3] Appeals by the Museum to the court to permit the use of income from the Marlatt, Wade, and Severance purchase funds for building purposes for a three-year period were equally successful and had the specific endorsement of the trustees of the Kelley Foundation.[4]

In 1953 the Hanna Fund had pledged up to $1,500,000 to match further contributions from other sources, and in 1955 the Hanna matching fund had been raised to $2,000,000. Meantime estimates of the cost of a new wing rose steadily as plans for its construction matured. From an original estimate of $3,000,000 to $4,000,000 the figure rose to $5,500,000 by November 1955, with $4,600,000 either in hand or pledged, and to more than $9,000,000 in 1957.[5] New appeals to the trustees of the Huntington and Hanna funds resulted in further pledges of financial assistance. To provide for the expansion of the Museum and a large parking lot north of the Museum for visitors, Cleveland's City Council, without debate, transferred four acres of Wade Park to the Board of Trustees.[6]

In 1953 J. Byers Hays and Paul C. Ruth were selected as the architects and the firm of Sam W. Emerson as general contractors for the addition to the Museum. Hays made intensive studies of some thirty museums in this country and abroad before he prepared his model for the new building. The need to harmonize the new structure with the old created problems both of a functional and aesthetic nature. Much remodeling and redecorating of the old building was required, as well as improvement in lighting to permit the proper blending of daylight and artificial light in the galleries. Stacks to hold 80,-000 volumes were planned for the library. Air conditioning to circulate 475,000 cubic feet of air per hour seemed essential, as well as electric equipment to clean the air.[7] Reminiscent of the legal complications which had to be surmounted in 1913 when the Museum was incorporated, a supplemental agreement had to be worked out between the Museum and the Huntington and Kelley interests when the new wing was built, and a quit-claim deed was executed in May 1958 for land needed for the new addition and still technically under the control of these two foundations.

The addition of the new wing doubled the size of the Museum, added twenty-three galleries to the existing seventeen and increased the galleries for the display of paintings from seven to fifteen. Ground was broken for the new wing in 1955, with a golden shovel, so the newspapers reported. The cornerstone was laid July 14, 1956. Beginning April 1, 1957, the Museum had to be closed for nearly a year for reasons of safety while construction was in progress. In the interim, the May Show and a much abbreviated program of the department of education were housed in the old building of the Institute of Art, which by this time had moved into its new home opposite the Museum.

140

The problems encountered by the architects, building contractors, and the Museum staff were too numerous and complicated to discuss here. For the most part they were not unusual in a building operation of such magnitude. The only untoward incident during the period of construction was a fire in the early stages of the operation which destroyed six construction sheds and tools of the Emerson Company.[8] The Board of Trustees put associate director Lee in charge of the difficult task of rearranging the contents and facilities of the Museum for a structure twice the size of the old.

In March 1958 the reconstructed Museum was ready for reopening to the public. Cleveland, long known as a giant city of iron, steel and shipping, now experienced a rebirth as a giant of the museum world. Its enlarged Museum covered an area of 80,000 square feet. Although the Metropolitan of New York was much larger and had a roof area of seven and a half acres, the Cleveland institution now ranked with the great museums of the country. A 62-page book, prepared by Milliken to mark the dedication of the new wing, contained 35 color and 75 black and white reproductions of some of the Cleveland Museum's most precious treasures.

The architects succeeded in blending the imposing structures in which these treasures were housed into a harmonious unit. In the new wing, dark red granite from Minnesota was used for the base and light gray from Maine for the upper portion to blend with the white Georgian marble of the old building, now mellowed after 43 years into a soft gray. A glass and stainless steel corridor linked the new wing to the old.

On March 4, 1958, the president and the director of the Museum cut the ribbon which opened the reconstructed Museum to the public. Mrs. R. Henry Norweb served as the chairman of an inaugural committee which planned the dedicatory exercises. At a subscription luncheon in a downtown hotel more than a thousand guests heard James J. Rorimer, a native son of Cleveland and director of the Metropolitan Museum of New York, discourse on "The Place of the Museum in the Community." Unfortunately, Whiting, the first director of the Museum, was ill at his home in Massachusetts and could not attend. At the luncheon, a Golden Book containing the names of all donors but without indicating the amounts contributed, and the annual membership list as well, was distributed as a memento of the occasion.

On the eve of the formal opening of the new wing the trustees entertained out-of-town guests and local patrons of the Museum at a dinner at the Union Club where 463 guests listened to speeches by the president of the New York Metropolitan Museum, the directors of the municipal museums of St. Louis and Hartford, Connecticut, a representative of UNESCO, and Milliken, who would retire as director of the Cleveland Museum in less than a month. Meantime, there was an exhibit of the Leonard C. Hanna Jr. collection of French impressionists and other treasures that had come to the Museum from his estate.

The dedication of the new wing received national and international coverage in the press and in the art journals. *Life, Look, Newsweek,* and other leading American magazines covered the inaugural ceremonies with photographs and narrative accounts; art journals like *Museum News* and *Art News* of New York ran feature stories on the Museum, and in Paris the *Gazette des Beaux Arts* gave more than passing attention to what its editors regarded as an event of international importance in the world of art.

By a sad stroke of fate, the man who had done most to finance the building of the new wing and whose final bequests were to insure the future of the Museum as one of the major art centers of the world could not participate in the dedicatory ceremonies. On July 14, 1956, Leonard C. Hanna had made his last visit to The Cleveland Museum of Art to take part in the laying of the cornerstone for the new wing. He died October 5 of the following year.

Hanna's father was one of the organizers of the M. A. Hanna Company, one of Cleveland's industrial giants in the field of iron ore, coal, pig iron, and shipping. Leonard's uncle was Ohio's famous Senator Marcus A. Hanna. A graduate of Yale in 1913 and a devoted alumnus of his alma mater, young Hanna served his apprenticeship in business with the Republic Iron and Steel Company in Youngstown, Ohio, and Birmingham, Alabama. In 1917 he was admitted to partnership in the M. A. Hanna Company, but he was never very active in the business which provided him with much of his great wealth.

Hanna's primary interest was in art, music, the theatre, sports, and a long list of minor and major philanthropies. In 1941 he took the lead in incorporating the Hanna Fund which supported many charitable, educational and cultural activities, and of which he, Harold Clark, and the late Howard M. Hanna were the original trustees. The latter was succeeded by Lewis Blair Williams, who had long been instrumental in handling the Museum's investments. The fund gave to more than 35 institutions, including Western Reserve University, Karamu, the Cleveland Play House, hospitals, medical schools, and other private and public charities. With his mother, Hanna gave Hanna House to the University Hospitals, and later he made a generous contribution to the Howard M. Hanna Memorial Pavilion for the care of the mentally ill.

In 1925 Hanna began giving reproductions of famous paintings to the Cleveland public schools. His own private art collection, mostly the work of French impressionist and post-impressionist artists, was valued between $1,500,000 and $2,000,000. At the time of his death he was president and treasurer of the Hanna Fund, a trustee and vice-president of The Cleveland Museum of Art, and a trustee of the Huntington Art and Polytechnic Trust. A bachelor, a man of strong likes and dislikes (which included a special disgust with Prohibition and the New Deal), Hanna shunned publicity, sincerely believed in the obligations of wealthy men to serve the public interest in a society of free enterprise, and was deeply concerned with helping humanity and stressing the development of aesthetic values in our American civilization.

Shortly after Hanna's death it became known that his residual estate would go to the Museum, half to be used for purchases and half for endowment. Clark, who had been Hanna's attorney since 1917 and a close friend, was the executor of the will. There was much speculation in the newspapers about the size of the estate. *The Cleveland Press* reported that it would exceed $10,000,000; *The Akron Beacon Journal* believed the Museum alone would get twice that amount, but all agreed that the bequest probably was the largest single gift ever made to an American museum.[9] *Life* devoted four and a half pages to an account of the Hanna bequest, and it was noted in foreign publications as well. Meantime estimates of its size continued to grow.

The executor's final accounting to the Probate Court of Painesville, Ohio, in the county in which Hanna had his country home revealed that the residue of the estate destined for the Museum totaled between $33,000,000 and $34,000,000. In addition, the Museum received Hanna's private art collection, valued at a minimum of $1,500,000 and purchased with the thought that its ultimate destination would be the Cleveland Museum. Earlier gifts from the Hanna fund for the construction of the new wing of the Museum had amounted to another $4,500,000. At the close of 1964 the Museum carried the Leonard C. Hanna Jr. Bequest on its books at a book value of $30,346,570.49. The market value of the common stocks alone exceeded this figure by many millions. Although the Cleveland Museum's endowment still was less than that of

144

New York's Metropolitan, Cleveland now took second place among American museums, displacing the Boston Museum, which dropped to third position. It would not have been inappropriate to name the new wing of the Cleveland Museum for its most generous donor. Leonard Hanna did not want it so.

While a steadily growing museum constantly requires additional funds for purchases, operations and expansion, the unprecedented Hanna bequest assured the future of the Museum as one of the greatest institutions of its kind in the art world. When Jeptha Wade gave the land on which the Museum eventually was built, he expressed the hope that it would be used "for the benefit of all the people forever." That hope has been realized abundantly. Built largely by wealthy and public-spirited donors, it stands today as a proud creation which the people of Cleveland regard as their own. Its development as a cultural catalyst for the entire community has been remarkably fast. Without a dollar of public money the Museum was built by a civic-minded group from various walks of life whose benefactions made them and their fellow citizens increasingly art-conscious. Along with the Cleveland Orchestra in Severance Hall the Museum is the most widely known institution among the 29 educational, religious, cultural, and medical institutions which constitute University Circle, "the cultural heart of Cleveland." As early as the 1920's, Whiting, the first director of the Museum, had discussed the possibility of a cooperative enterprise which would make the University Circle development one of the beauty spots of the nation.

The Cleveland Museum, in its first fifty years, has become a vital element in the cultural and educational life of Greater Cleveland. To hundreds of school children and to the most sophisticated scholars in the field of art it has much to offer, for it seeks to serve all the people. Most of the thousands who visit its galleries year in and year out are not scholars or the

145

tutored in art but men, women, and children, native and foreign-born Americans, who are eager to be enlightened and who get genuine pleasure from what they see. The Museum has quickened their cultural life in ways that defy description. Its expanding membership rolls and the hundreds of thousands who visit its galleries annually testify to the Museum's close relation with the community it serves.

These fifty years in the life of The Cleveland Museum of Art have been years of bold adventure. They represent a unique achievement in combining the material wealth, the creative energy, and the high sense of obligation of Cleveland's citizens with a basic desire to develop and enrich their artistic tastes.

The function of the Museum is to preserve, to exhibit, and to promote education and research. Its art objects serve as a means of public education but beyond that they can produce delight and even exaltation for the individual who observes them, introduce him to new and pleasurable sensations, and develop in him better standards of appreciation and judgment which in turn will gradually influence the whole community. This satisfying experience with the art treasures of the world, accumulated over the long years as man emerged from savagery to civilization, not only adds to the enjoyment of life but also can enrich man's sense of values about the whole human enterprise. The Museum remains the guardian of man's artistic heritage, the voice which echoes the eloquent messages of the past for present and future generations.

146

Notes to the Text

CHAPTER I

[1] Beverly W. Bond, Jr., *The Foundations of Ohio*, Vol. I: *History of Ohio*, ed., Carl Wittke (Columbus, 1941), p. 366.

[2] See Edmund H. Chapman, *Cleveland: Village to Metropolis* (Cleveland, 1964), pp. 140, 143.

[3] See Alfred Mowett, *A Brief History of Troop A, 107th Regiment of Cavalry, Ohio National Guard* (Cleveland, 1923).

[4] For further details on Cleveland's history, see James B. Whipple, "Cleveland in Conflict, a Study in Urban Adolescence, 1876–1900" (unpublished doctoral dissertation, Western Reserve University, 1951); Harlan Hatcher, *The Western Reserve* (Indianapolis, 1949) and *A Century of Iron and Men* (Indianapolis, 1950); Philip D. Jordan, *The History of Ohio*, Vol. V: *Ohio Comes of Age, 1873–1900*, ed., Carl Wittke (Columbus, 1943); Charles E. Kennedy, *Fifty Years of Cleveland, 1875–1925* (Cleveland, 1925); and William G. Rose, *Cleveland, the Making of a City* (Cleveland, 1950).

CHAPTER II

[1] See Donald R. MacKenzie, "Collections and Exhibits, Early Ohio Painters, Cincinnati, 1830–1850," in *Ohio History,* LXXIII, 111–118; and by the same author, "The Itinerant Artist in Early Ohio," *ibid.,* pp. 41–46; and "The Pre-War Years," *ibid.,* pp. 254–262; also Edna M. Clark, *Ohio Art and Artists* (Richmond, 1932), especially pp. 73–101.

[2] Elbert J. Benton, *Cultural Story of an American City, Cleveland* (Cleveland, 1944), Part II.

[3] I am heavily indebted here to Nancy Coe's "The History of the Collecting of European Paintings and Drawings in the City of

Cleveland" (Master's thesis, Oberlin College, 1959). See also Edna M. Clark, pp. 124–133, and references to the Hurlbut and Worthington collections in Edward Strahan, *The Art Treasures of America* (Philadelphia, 1879).

[4] *Cleveland Leader,* October 4, 1865.

[5] July 16, 1877.

[6] Arthur H. Auten, "Archibald M. Willard, The Painter of *The Spirit of '76*" (Master's thesis, Western Reserve University, 1960).

[7] *Cleveland Leader,* December 4, 1875.

[8] E. W. Palmer, "Early Days of Art in Cleveland" (manuscript in the Western Reserve Historical Society).

[9] *Cleveland Leader and Herald,* May 30, 1877.

[10] Vol. I, No. 11 (November 1883), p. 132.

[11] *Ibid.,* No. 5.

[12] *Cleveland Leader,* March 27, 1877.

[13] Quoted in S. E. Morison and H. S. Commager, *The Growth of the American Republic* (New York, 1962), II, 130–131.

[14] *Cleveland Herald,* October 15, 1878.

[15] *Ibid.,* November 2, 1878.

[16] See Coe.

CHAPTER III

[1] *Cleveland Leader,* October 31, 1866; *Wächter am Erie,* May 5, 1866.

[2] *Cleveland Leader,* August 24, 1866.

[3] During the mayoralty campaign, the following parody of the poem by Robert Burns, signed "A Workingman," appeared in *The Cleveland Leader,* April 2, 1873:

> John Huntington, my Joe John
> When first we were acquaint
> Ye were a toiling laborer,
> Which now all know you ain't.
>
> *   *   *
>
> We toiled and strove together
>
> *   *   *
>
> No one e're found your purse or hand
> Closed to another's woe,
> Ye always by the poor did stand,
> John Huntington, my Joe.

[4] I have benefited greatly from the preliminary and unpublished research done by John J. Horton on the founders of the Museum.

[5] *Plain Dealer,* December 22, 1957.

[6] For Kelley's Island, see George C. Huntington, "Historical Sketch of Kelley's Island," *The Firelands Pioneer,* IV (June 1863), 30–49.

[7] See Trustees Minutes, December 23, 1915. The Report of the Trustees of the Hurlbut Estate (Clark, Hord, and Horton) gives a complete list of the art objects. Probate Court, Docket L, No. 1466. Dated November 20, 1933.

[8] *Weekly Gazette and Comet,* Baton Rouge, June 30, 1866.

[9] See Wade's 19-page autobiography (1889), a manuscript in the Western Reserve Historical Society. For details on Wade's role in the telegraph business, see Robert F. Thompson, *Wiring a Continent: The History of the Telegraph Industry in the United States, 1832–1866* (Princeton, 1947); and Russell H. Anderson, "Jeptha Wade and the Cleveland and Cincinnati Telegraph Company," *Ohio Archaeological and Historical Quarterly,* LVIII (January 1949), 80–93; and William F. Zornow, "Jeptha H. Wade in California, Beginning the Transcontinental Telegraph," *California Historical Society Quarterly,* XXIX (1950), 345–346.

[10] *Plain Dealer,* March 8, 1926.

CHAPTER IV

[1] See Case No. 125083, Cuyahoga County Common Pleas Court, December 6, 1911.

[2] *Plain Dealer Magazine,* June 14, 1908.

[3] Memorandum of a conversation between Harold T. Clark and Henry W. Kent, Fairfield, Connecticut, November 9, 1936.

[4] See Winifred E. Howe, *The History of the Metropolitan Museum of Art* (New York, 1913), I, 305–307; II, 151, 164–165.

[5] December 3, 1908.

[6] *Lakewood Post,* July 31, 1924; *Art News,* April 2, 1926.

[7] July 24, 1928; also *Cleveland Press,* July 21, 1928.

[8] *Cleveland News,* September 13, October 11, 1928.

[9] *Ibid.,* August 10, 1928.

[10] *Plain Dealer,* June 13, 1930.

[11] *Ibid.,* March 4, 1930.

[12] René Gimpel, French art dealer, visited Cleveland in 1923. He described Whiting as "un homme froid, au coeur chaud" and young

Milliken as full of irresistible "enthusiasme juvenile." René Gimpel, *Journal d'un collectionneur, marchand de tableaux* (Paris, 1963), pp. 235–236.

CHAPTER V

[1] For the Chicago Artists' Exhibition and Art Sale, see *The Sketch Book* (Chicago), Vol. V, no. 6 (February 1906). In 1910 Chicago had 140 "Friends of Art" who agreed to subscribe $200 a year for five years for the purchase of work by American artists. See N. H. Carpenter, "How the Art Institute of Chicago Has Increased Its Usefulness," *American Magazine of Art*, January 1917, pp. 100–103; *The Collections Illustrated* (Chicago Institute of Art, 1910), p. 25.

[2] Milliken to Simkhovitch, May 2, 1951.

[3] Trustees Minutes, February 8, 1939.

[4] *Plain Dealer*, May 12, 1963.

[5] See *New York World*, May 16, 1926; *Boston Transcript*, May 14, June 7, 1926; *Christian Science Monitor*, June 9, 1926.

[6] May 11, 1926.

[7] *Plain Dealer*, May 19, 1923.

[8] May 23, 1926.

[9] *Cleveland Press*, May 2, 1935.

[10] May 4, 1945.

[11] May 1958.

[12] *Plain Dealer*, May 21, 1958.

[13] *Cleveland Press*, May 13, 1959.

[14] McBride to Lee, May 7, 1959; Lee to McBride, May 12, 1959.

[15] June 2, 1962.

[16] *Plain Dealer*, February 20, 1961, and July 7, 1962.

[17] See *Cleveland Press*, May 10, 1960, and May 8, 1961; *Plain Dealer*, June 4, 1961.

[18] *Plain Dealer*, April 26, 1928.

[19] *Ibid.*, May 8, 1950.

[20] *Cleveland News*, May 8, 1954; also May 6, 1955.

[21] *Cleveland Press*, June 15, 1963.

CHAPTER VI

[1] For further details on the educational work of the Museum, see Thomas Munro and Jane Grimes, *Educational Work at The Cleve-*

land Museum of Art (Cleveland, 1952) and Munro, *Art Education, Its Philosophy and Psychology* (New York, 1956), Chapter XII.

[2] For a bibliography through 1964, see *Journal of Aesthetics and Art Criticism,* XXIII (Fall 1964), 7–11.

[3] See also, Max Rieser, "Thomas Munro's Position in American Aesthetics," *Journal of Aesthetics and Art Criticism,* XXIII (Fall 1964), 13–20.

[4] *Bulletin,* October 1939 and February 1943.

CHAPTER VII

[1] See Winifred E. Howe, *A History of the Metropolitan Museum of Art* (New York, 1946), II, 144; *American Magazine of Art,* VIII (January 1917), 102.

[2] Whiting to Ralph King, July 17, 1919.

[3] See *American Organist,* March 1934. The article was reprinted in pamphlet form by The Cleveland Museum of Art.

[4] *Plain Dealer,* January 21, 22, and April 23, 1923.

[5] *Plain Dealer,* February 23, 1928; *Press,* February 24, 1928.

[6] *Plain Dealer,* April 25, 1932.

[7] *Ibid.,* May 14, 22, 1960.

CHAPTER VIII

[1] *Bulletin,* May 1926, Part I.

[2] The Cleveland collection is discussed in Frits Lugt, *Les Marques de Collections de Dessins et d'Estampes,* Supplement (The Hague, 1956), pp. 67–68.

[3] Francis to Parsons, February 3, 1939.

[4] See Milliken's article in *Art News,* February 1951, pp. 30–37, 62.

[5] *Plain Dealer,* February 17, 1931.

[6] For detailed descriptions, see *Bulletin,* November 1930, January and February 1931; and Milliken: "The Guelph Treasure," in *American Magazine of Art,* Vol. XXII, no. 3, pp. 163–173.

[7] *Frankfurter Zeitung,* August 12, 1930; *Frankfurter Handelszeitung,* August 12, 1930; *Deutsche Zeitung* (Berlin), September 30, 1930; *Münchener Neueste Nachrichten,* January 30, 1931; see also *New York World,* November 30, 1930, and *New York Evening Post,* November 29, 1930.

[8] While there was general approval of the purchase at the time, a member of the Advisory Council, in 1939, protested that the "excessive expenditures" had handicapped the Museum in making other purchases, in American and contemporary art which might have had a wider appeal to the citizens of Cleveland. McBride to Milliken, April 3, 1939.

[9] *Bulletin,* June 1936; *Cleveland Press,* June 6, 27, 1936; *Plain Dealer,* June 6, 1936; see also the article by Milliken in *Art Digest,* X (July 1, 1936).

[10] The *Bulletin* for June 1941 lists major accessions.

[11] *Plain Dealer,* January 6, 1951; *New York Times,* February 4, 1951.

[12] *Plain Dealer,* November 2, 1933.

[13] Trustees Minutes, May 19, and November 3, 1948; *Cleveland Press,* September 22, 1948; *Plain Dealer,* October 10, 1948.

[14] *Plain Dealer,* December 8, 1961.

[15] *Ibid.,* February 28, 1947.

[16] *Bulletin,* January 1920.

[17] March 11, 1923.

[18] See Lee's article in *Apollo,* LXXVIII (December 1963).

[19] *Bulletin,* November 1946.

[20] See also on Cleveland's immigrants, Wellington G. Fordyce, "Immigrant Colonies in Cleveland," *Ohio Archaeological and Historical Quarterly,* October 1936, pp. 320–340; and "Immigrant Institutions in Cleveland," *ibid.,* April 1938, pp. 87–103.

[21] *Cleveland Press,* February 27, 1928.

[22] *Ibid.,* November 10, 1933.

[23] *Plain Dealer,* May 5, 1950.

[24] *Ibid.,* January 8, 1951.

CHAPTER IX

[1] Trustees Minutes, March 9, 1962.

[2] *Cleveland News,* September 23, 1946.

[3] Trustees Minutes, December 1955.

[4] *Ibid.,* January 22, 1919.

[5] See Henry S. Francis on Milliken's career, in *Bulletin,* April 1958, pp. 99–107.

[6] *Melbourne Sun,* May 19, 1959.

[7] Trustees Minutes, February 25, April 23, 1915.

[8] *Ibid.,* May 7, 1947.

[9] See also Marie Kirkwood, "The Fine Art of Restoring Masterpieces from the Past," *Plain Dealer Magazine,* December 25, 1960.

[10] *New York Herald-Tribune,* February 15, 1925; *Christian Science Monitor,* February 21, 1925.

[11] Milliken to Siple (director of the Cincinnati Art Museum), October 20, 1937.

[12] For details, see Trustees Minutes, especially, July 15, 1946; May 7, August 1, December 19, 1947; April 22, June 2, November 7, 1950; December 11, 1956; February 6, 1963.

CHAPTER X

[1] *Bulletin of the Pennsylvania Museum,* April 1905, pp. 37–38.

[2] Milliken to Banks, February 4, 1930.

[3] Milliken to Parsons, January 30, 1934.

[4] Trustees Minutes, June 28, 1945.

[5] *Ibid.,* December 22, 1921.

[6] *Plain Dealer,* January 13, 1936.

[7] *Cleveland News,* December 28, 1921.

[8] *Ibid.,* March 23, 1931.

[9] Parsons to Milliken, March 22, 1934.

[10] Parsons to Milliken, May 22, 1953.

[11] Parsons to Howard, June 1, 1925, and December 7, 1926; also Parsons to Francis, September 8, 1932.

[12] See Charles F. Ramus, art critic of the *Cleveland News,* February 23, 1930.

[13] Registrar's Report, 1951.

[14] See, e.g., *Time,* February 24, 1961; *New York Times,* February 26, 1961.

[15] Letter to Lee, October 29, 1962.

[16] Trustees Minutes, November 5, 1952.

[17] Parsons to Milliken, August 19, 1928; also July 14, 1955; and Walter Lusetti, *Alceo Dossena, Scultore* (Rome, 1955).

[18] Bill of Sale, May 14, 1927.

[19] Parsons to Whiting, April 17, 1927.

[20] Parsons to Whiting, December 31, 1927, and April 10, 1928; Hirsch to Whiting, November 4, 1927, and Trustees Minutes, May 31, 1928.

[21] Parsons to Whiting, March 11, 1924.

[22] *Bulletin,* March 1925.

[23] *Ibid.,* April 1929, pp. 66–67. Photographs of the two objects once

owned by The Cleveland Museum of Art are in Lusetti's *Dossena*.

24 November 24, 1928.

25 See also *Art News,* December 8, 1928; *Literary Digest,* December 22, 1928; *Cleveland News,* November 23, 1928, and *Plain Dealer,* November 25, 1928.

26 *London Sunday Dispatch,* September 27, 1959. French papers also noted the sale: *L'Espoir* (Nice), September 28, 1959.

27 See also *Time,* January 12, 1962, and *New York Times,* January 9, 1962.

28 Olga Hale-Brown to Lee, February 3, 1962.

29 Trustees Minutes, October 26, 1929; *Bulletin,* October 1928, December 1929; *New York Times,* November 10, 1929.

30 Trustees Minutes, January 23, 1950, and *Cleveland News,* December 29, 1950.

31 *Plain Dealer,* November 14, 15, 1960; Trustees Minutes, December 19, 1960.

32 Trustees Minutes, October 25, 1939.

33 See also *Plain Dealer,* June 19, 30, July 24, 1955; *Cleveland Press,* July 6, 1955; *Cleveland News,* June 18, July 7, August 1, 1955.

34 See *Toledo Blade,* December 29, 1957, November 3, 6, 8, 1959; *Plain Dealer,* November 3, 1959; and Fernand Auberjonois, "The Missing Mourners of Dijon," *Horizon,* October 1958.

35 Milton W. Brown, *The Story of the Armory Show* (New York, 1963).

36 *Cleveland News,* November 5, 1922, and October 26, 1924; *Cleveland Times,* October 31, 1924.

37 September 20, 25, 1931.

38 *Plain Dealer,* January 12, 1937.

39 *Pittsburgh Telegram,* November 21, 1939.

40 *Bulletin,* March 1947.

41 See also *Cleveland News,* November 11, 1958; *Cleveland Press,* November 15, 1958.

42 Trustees Minutes, January 15, 1960.

43 *Plain Dealer,* March 13, April 29, 1962.

44 "Disgusted Homo" to Lee, February 1964.

CHAPTER XI

1 For more details, see Carl Wittke, *German-Americans and the World War* (Columbus, 1936).

2 April 1918.

[3] Whitlock to Whiting, December 5, 1914.

[4] Whiting to Parsons, January 30, 1915.

[5] *Plain Dealer*, September 22, 1918.

[6] *Cleveland Press*, January 4, 1930.

[7] Trustees Minutes, May 26, 1933; June 21, 1934.

[8] *Ibid.*, October 20, December 6, 1932.

[9] *Cleveland News*, June 5, 1932.

[10] Trustees Minutes, November 23, 1933.

[11] *Plain Dealer*, July 19, 1932; *Cleveland Press*, July 30, 1932.

[12] *Cleveland Press*, August 5, 1933; *Plain Dealer*, August 6, 1933.

[13] *Cleveland Press*, August 17, 1934. Similar markets were held in other cities.

[14] *Pittsburgh Press*, November 19, 1936. For a discussion of the federal projects, see Dixon Wecter, *The Age of the Great Depression, 1929–1941* (New York, 1948), pp. 267–271.

[15] For more details, see *Plain Dealer*, December 16, 31, 1933, and November 12, 1934; *Cleveland News*, December 2, 15, 1933, and March 16, 1934; *Cleveland Press*, December 2, 11, 1933; *Toledo Blade*, December 16, 1933.

[16] *Plain Dealer*, April 10, May 1, June 12, 1935; *Cleveland News*, February 18, 1935.

[17] *Cleveland News*, February 8, 1936.

[18] Milliken to Parsons, October 10, 1935; *Plain Dealer*, February 20, 1937.

[19] *Cleveland News*, June 25, 1938.

[20] Trustees Minutes, October 25, 1939.

[21] *Ibid.*, July 14, 1941.

[22] *Cleveland News*, January 26, 1940.

[23] *Jewish Independent*, July 9, 1943.

[24] Trustees Minutes, September 29, 1950; January 18, 1951.

[25] *Ibid.*, November 9, 1936.

[26] Milliken to Simkhovitch, February 6, 1951.

CHAPTER XII

[1] *Bulletin*, June 1957.

[2] Milliken to Parsons, January 19, 1955.

[3] Trustees Minutes, April 28, 1955; *Plain Dealer*, July 12, 1953; *Cleveland News*, August 12, 1953.

[4] *Bulletin*, June 1957.

[5] Trustees Minutes, November 21, 1955; July 29, 1957.

[6] *Plain Dealer,* February 22, 1955.

[7] *Bulletin,* Annual Report 1958, p. 142. The Museum's *Golden Book* (1958) gives the layout of the building in detail.

[8] *Plain Dealer,* July 7, 1955.

[9] *Cleveland Press,* October 9, 1957; *Akron Beacon Journal,* January 11, 1958; *Plain Dealer,* January 11, 1958.

Index